From Risk to Resilience

A Journey with Heart for Our Children, Our Future

by E. Timothy Burns

Marco Polo Publishers

Printed in the United States of America

Editing, typesetting, page layout, and cover designed by
Bill and Pat Baldwin, Helmsman Publications. Proof-
reading by Bob Crow, Helmsman Publications.

The Marco Polo Group
17194 Preston Road, Suite 123
Dallas, Texas 75248-1203

ISBN 1-56374-017-6
Library of Congress Catalog Card Number 94-76962

Dedication

For my daughters, Séa, Ashley, and
Megan and for all our children,
everywhere,

"Keepers of the dream."

Acknowledgments

A book is never the work of one individual. This one would never have come into being without:

First and foremost, the beauty of trees from a generous and beautiful planet for the pages on which it is written.

Editors and producers, Bill and Pat Baldwin, whose tireless and committed work, consummate skills, and vast love of excellence shines forth on every page. I treasure our work relationship and friendship.

Brian Dugan whose spirit of collaboration, knowledge of the fascinating worlds of marketing and service, and abundance of good cheer makes each and every contact a neat event.

Nan Henderson, whose understanding of and enthusiasm for the concept of resilience helped to launch our Resilient Child Training Institute.

Nan Rosendahl, colleague, friend, and continual source of support.

The many authors, books, articles, teachers, colleagues, students, workshop participants, and others who have enthusiastically shared their experiences, knowledge, ideas, and wisdom on the topics at hand. It is really impossible to separate their ideas from my own after all the time spent reading, thinking, talking, and teaching about them. I have, however, attempted to provide accurate representations of and credit for these ideas wherever possible in the book.

My parents Edward and Beatrice, who, by the example of their lives, offer special teachings in the ways of love, unconditional regard, and the power of surrender to the vicissitudes of life.

And, finally, those without whom this book would only have been so many words—my family. My beautiful, creative wife Zana, both container for and provider of my deepest love and support. My daughter Séa, beautiful and resilient, who brings a wonderful son-in-law, Murray, into our lives, daughter Ashley, who arrives on the threshold of adolescence with such a glowing sense of self, and daughter Megan, whose laughter, wit and love of music lights up our home.

The solution of adult problems tomorrow depends upon the way we raise our children today. There is no greater insight into the future than recognizing when we save our children, we save ourselves.

— *Margaret Mead*

Foreword

by Bonnie Benard

Prevention Specialist, Resiliency Reseacher, and Author of *Fostering Resiliency in Kids: Protective Factors in the Family, School, and Community*

I want to say, "Thank you, Tim Burns, for writing *From Risk to Resilience*," both for me personally and for the prevention, education, and youth work fields. From a personal perspective, I feel "let off the hook." Tim says what I would want to say in the book I never seem to get around to writing, and he says it in such a compelling, understandable, and heartfelt style. Speaking for the "field," Tim's book is a valuable contribution for all the practitioners, both direct service providers and policy makers, who are concerned with promoting healthy child development and, thereby, preventing the inter-related problems of alcohol and other drug abuse, delinquency and violence, school failure, and teen pregnancy, especially in the increasing numbers of children and youth growing up in high-risk settings. Tim's perspective, that I and a growing number of researchers and practitioners share, is that healthy child development results from family, school, and community environments that support and elicit the innate resiliency, the "self-righting mechanisms" within every person.

From Risk to Resilience draws on and integrates several fields of research that support the movement from a risk to a resiliency focus in education and human services. It cogently crafts the case for moving beyond a pathology approach that focuses on the deficits of children and families to an empowerment perspective that concentrates on and engages their strengths. Grounding his discussion in child development research, Tim provides a framework for inter-relating the work of major theorists like Joseph Chilton Pierce, Piaget, Erikson, Maslow, Kohlberg, and Rudolph Steiner.

Overlaying this foundation, Tim weaves the findings of cognitive science on how we learn and discoveries of the exciting new field of psychoneuroimmunology that validates the role of the mind in stress reduction and health promotion. Confirming all of this research, Tim discusses the finding from longitudinal, prospective, and even community-wide studies into human resilience that verify the environmental protective factors that buffer the growing child from environmental risks and adversity: caring relationships in the family, school, and community environments that convey positive expectations to children, youth, and families and that, consequently, offer ongoing opportunities for meaningful participation.

The closing discussion of "The Resilient Care Provider" strikes at the heart of how we can move *From Risk to Resilience*. As Tim states, "...children will grow in health and resilience only as we, the adult care providers, identify, appreciate, and indeed demonstrate our own resiliency." Real change comes from the inside-out, from loving and accepting ourselves. When Tim talks about the importance of identifying our individual gifts and following our passions, I'm reminded of the words of Nora Zeale Hurston's resilient character, Janey, in *Their Eyes Were Watching God*: "Two things everybody's got tuh do fuh themselves. They got tuh go tuh God, and they got tuh find out about livin' fuh themselves."

Thanks again, Tim, for moving us forward on our journey *From Risk to Resilience*.

Table of Contents

Prologue

Prologue

This is an important book. Not because I authored it, nor because of the manner in which it is written. It is important because of the ideas contained within it and because of the possibility that you, the reader, can find and rejoice in a renewed vision of childhood.

All this from ideas? I believe so. Victor Hugo said it best: "Nothing is so powerful as an idea whose time has come." And the concept of resilience—the idea that under certain circumstances children *can* bounce back from virtually *any* adversity, is indeed a powerful and welcome idea.

Resilience is an idea that should go far towards moving us away from the useful, but increasingly frustrating and limited, model of young people exclusively "at risk" (damaged, defective, and dysfunctional—in need of rehabilitation, remediation and repair.) It aligns us with what knowing psychologists have been speaking about for years—that young people grow best and fastest when we work with their strengths. They do not grow as well when we overly remediate, focusing mainly on their weaknesses.

The reality is that children, teenagers, and adults do bounce back from adversity —even a great deal of adversity. This is nothing new. What is new is the way in which this marvelous and universal human quality has been carefully and systematically observed and documented by an ever-expanding group of intelligent, well-trained, and sensitive researchers.

This book, then, represents a very small effort to bring these ideas—very few of which originated with me—to life for the people with whom I work, and others who show an interest. It is a book about the research and the ideas of others as I have understood, personalized, and taught them.

I must confess that I do not fancy myself a writer. Writing, for me, is a real labor—fulfilling, but never easy. I would almost always rather be doing something—anything—else. But in the end, I enjoy the satisfaction of knowing that others benefit from the final product.

Organizationally, the book is written in three sections. The first section describes the nature and origins of vulnerability and risk for children in our society. For those who may have read my earlier book, *Our Children, Our Future,* you will find this section to be a good review and a significant clarification of the themes in that book. In short, this section details the outer and inner world of childhood today in response to two powerful forces producing the greatest vulnerability in the highest number of young people in any society to date.

The second section takes the reader from vulnerability and risk to the nature of resilience. It is an examination of specific observations and discoveries related to the timely notion of what helps children beat the odds and overcome adversity. It includes a variety of suggested strategies and tactics taken from research.

The last section focuses on the special role that we, as adults, play in fostering resilience in children. If we neglect ourselves and focus exclusively on the children, we will miss a most important point about how children learn. It has been said, and I believe it is true, that ninety-five percent of all human learning is based upon modeling. We are the model for our children and this section describes the manner by which we can retain our own resiliency and model it effectively.

Introduction

Introduction

Making a Difference in an Indifferent World

There is a wonderful story about a little boy walking along a sandy beach, gently picking up starfish and lovingly tossing them back into the ocean. A man walked up to him and asked what he was doing. The boy said he was getting them back into the water before they died. Upon hearing this, the man appeared astonished and pointed at the vast expanse of beach, saying "You'll never make a difference. There are thousands of starfish out here."

Looking down at the starfish he held in his hands, the boy responded, "It will make a difference to this one," as he placed it back into the sea.

This touching story serves as a metaphor for what has been happening to children and young persons in our society over the last forty years. Like so many starfish washed up on a beach to languish, an increased number of our young have been struggling and literally dying for lack of attention, connectedness, and meaning in their lives.

One has only to look at Figure 1, "One Day in the Lives of American Children," to get an immediate picture of how bad things have become. This list presents the dismal reality of today's childhood, in what is still considered one of the world's richest and most powerful nations.

7

17,051	women get pregnant
2,795	of them are teenagers
1,106	teenagers have abortions
372	teenagers miscarry
1,295	teenagers give birth
689	babies are born to women who have had inadequate prenatal care
719	babies are born at low birthweight
129	babies are born at very low birthweight
67	babies die before one month of life
105	babies die before their first birthday
27	children die from poverty
10	children die from guns
30	children are wounded by guns
6	teenagers commit suidice
135,000	children bring a gun to school
7,742	teens become sexually active
623	teenagers get syphilis or gonorrhea
211	children are arrested from drug abuse
437	children are arrested for drinking or drunken driving
1,512	teenagers drop out of school
1,849	children are abused or neglected
3,288	children run away from home
1,629	children are in adult jails
2,556	children are born out of wedlock
2,989	see their parents divorced
34,285	people lose jobs

Figure 1: One Day in the Lives of American Children
Adapted from Children 1990: A Report Card, Briefing
Book, and Action Primer; Children's Defense Fund,
Washington, D.C.

This does not bode well for our future. It is axiomatic that a society that does not care for its children cannot expect its children to care for it when they grow to be adults. Surely we are seeing the early results of this already in the form of increased violence and self-destructive behaviors exhibited by teenagers and young adults.

These statistics clearly point out the crisis of childhood today, which could well spawn a multitude of crises in the future. Some experts, for example, are saying that because of these deplorable conditions, fully forty percent of today's children may grow up to be non-productive adults—citizens who are more of a liability than an asset to society. Surely *no* society can expect to proceed in a positive manner with so many dysfunctional adults.

In reflecting upon the nature of this situation, I have come to regard with increased appreciation the Chinese interpretation of the word "crisis."

It is composed of two different characters and translates as "opportunity blowing on an ill wind." This conveys two meanings simultaneously. On the one hand, the word means *danger*. On the other hand, it means *opportunity*.

The first section of this book examines the dangers facing us in raising healthy and capable young persons, while the second section examines—in the light of the research on resilience and protective factors—the inherent opportunities, perhaps not fully appreciated until now.

With this in mind, let us begin our exploration by examining the nature of risk and vulnerability in today's society.

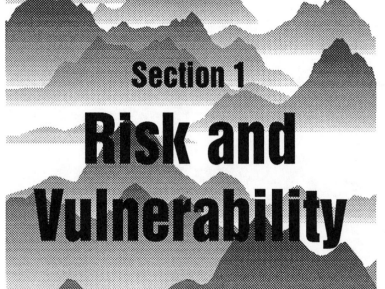

Section 1
Risk and Vulnerability

Chapter 1

Defining Risk

Before attempting to define and clarify the concept of risk, it is necessary to say that care must be taken in using this construct. Young people are at-risk only to the extent that their family, community and society are also at risk. In truth, they mirror, for better or for worse, the general conditions of society. Two potential problems stem from applying risk labels to young people. One is the tendency to "blame the victim," meaning that we blame young people for their condition without taking into consideration the broader context. Another is the very act of labeling can create a self-fulfilling prophecy. We will be returning to this idea later in the book.

We should start our discussion with a useful operational definition of young people at risk and understand some basic terminology. When we talk about "risk," "at-risk," and "high risk," exactly what are we describing?

We might define an "at-risk" young person as one who is facing two obstacles to full development. These are: the inner obstacles of unmet developmental needs, and the outer obstacles of increasing environmental stress. All children are going to go through their development with some unmet needs. In addition, all children, at various times, are going to face stress. There is, however, a situation occurring in our nation that is unique and, perhaps, unparalleled. I think, in some ways, it is expressed best by Urie Bronfenbrenner[1], who has been conducting research on at-risk youth in America for many years. His conclusion is that the current generation of young people—above and beyond all previous generations—is expressing the highest level of alienation and anomie of any generation in America.

Alienation refers to lack of certain essential conditions for human health. These are a lack of connectedness, a lack of bonding and/or a lack of belonging. *Anomie* refers to "normlessness"—not knowing what normal is. Those brought up not knowing what normal is, are growing up in a culture with no structure. For most of us, "normal" means a culture which has more or less clear values and consistent sanctions on what shouldn't be done, coupled with rewards and encouragement for what should be done. If I, as a young person, grow up in a culture without these anchors of normality, I grow up without any internalized structure for dealing with the problems that I face in my life. What Bronfenbrenner calls alienation and anomie can be paraphrased as follows:

If the child has too many unmet developmental needs, then that child is going to be more vulnerable to the experience of alienation; alienation from self, alienation from family, alienation from community. A child growing up alienated from self, family and community is more likely to experience development problems.

When Bronfenbrenner says *anomie*, he is describing a condition that is characterized by a lack of an internalized structure for dealing with problems—in other words—life skills, or coping skills. Life is stressful. How well we cope with and deal with that stress determines how well we do in life. It determines our ability to survive and also to thrive.

So what percentage of young people are "at-risk" in America today? According to most experts, the number is in the seventy to ninety percent range, depending upon the criteria being used. It is, however, important to note that an "at-risk" young person is not necessarily doomed to self-destructive behaviors. It *does* mean that he or she is more vulnerable to the effects of emotional, physical, or economic stress and pressure.

We also know that a young person who demonstrates risk behavior typically does so in a number of areas. For example, a recent study[2] of some 50,000 young people in grades six through twelve, was conducted in twenty-five states and approximately

125 smaller communities. One of the interesting findings of the Search Institute was that a teenager involved in one at-risk behavior is far more likely to be involved in one or more others. To illustrate this point, we look at Figure 2 and find the risk behavior of alcohol use. (In this study, alcohol use at a risk level was defined as binge drinking or frequent drinking.) Reading across the chart, we discover that the likelihood of this same hypothetical youngster engaging in illicit drug use is twenty-seven percent. His or her likelihood of experiencing depres-

Patterns of co-occurrence among at-risk behaviors

Percentage of risk in other, related areas

If at risk in this area	alcohol use	tobacco use	illicit drug use	sexuality	depression suicide	antisocial behavior	school	vehicle safety
•alcohol	•	42	27	70	33	49	23	86
•tobacco	66	•	35	77	39	53	26	85
•illicit drugs	72	60	•	84	46	61	32	88
•sexuality	49	34	22	•	34	41	19	77
•depression/ suicide	41	30	21	59	•	38	18	73
•antisocial behavior	54	37	24	64	34	•	22	82
•school	62	43	31	72	40	53	•	82
•vehicle safety	41	25	15	52	28	35	15	•

Source: The Troubled Journey: A Portrait of American Youth, Search Institute, Minneapolis, MN., 1990

Figure 2: Patterns of Co-occurrence of Risk Behaviors
Source: The Troubled Journey: A portrait of American Youth; *Search Institute, Minneapolis, MN, 1990*

Used by permission

sion, suicidal thoughts or attempts at suicide is thirty-three percent, for anti-social behavior, forty nine percent, and so forth.

Thus, "at-riskness" is a symptom or set of symptoms with underlying factors. Focusing exclusively on the symptom, for example by sending the teenager to a drug treatment facility, may result a very low success rate. The "univariate" approach to treating specific, individual symptoms may explain why, for example, only twelve to eighteen percent of teens who go for drug treatment succeed on the first attempt.

In the study, "The Troubled Journey: A Portrait of American Youth," the authors set out to determine the extent to which our youth are experiencing "well-being" (the best predictor of a low-risk lifestyle.) At the conclusion of the study, the authors found that *only ten percent* of the young persons studied could be said to be living in a state of well-being. That means that, to some degree or another, *ninety percent* are at-risk!

Clearly, "at-riskness" exists on a continuum from less to more and, as I said, describes a condition of vulnerability, not predictability. In fact, as we shall see, the entire concept of resil-

> *An operational definition of a high-risk young person might be this: we start with an "at-risk" person and we add three factors to it—lack of coping skills, lack of support, and poor self-concept.*

ience is *empowering* precisely because it helps us to rethink that notion of predictability as a consequence of vulnerability.

Since "at-riskness" seems to be a nearly universal fact of life in contemporary society, it is helpful to distinguish the "at-risk" child from the "high-risk" child.

Focusing on the High Risk Child

In light of the preponderance of vulnerable young people, it is easy to feel overwhelmed and discouraged. Fifty to one hundred years ago this was certainly not the case. It was probably the reverse. At that time, we could have said that about ten percent of the children were "at-risk" because of the factors that we will be studying. If alienation and anomie are almost universal, then we need something a little bit more focused to deal with—namely an operational definition of a *high-risk* young person.

An operational definition of a high-risk young person might be this: we start with an "at-risk" person and we add three factors to it—lack of coping skills, lack of support, and poor self-concept. Using this definition, it is possible that perhaps twenty-five percent of our young people would be considered at high-risk. Those would be young people who have unmet development needs; who have too much stress in their lives and who lack appropriate coping skills to face that stress. They do not have the support they need and they do not have the necessary self-esteem. They are represented in our drop-out, drug abuse, suicide, and pregnancy statistics.

Where do coping skills come from? How do young people learn to cope? How do we give them the kind of support that they need? What is it that builds self-esteem and self-concept? How do we support kids who are coping with stress in their lives? And what do we need to know about supporting and encouraging the appropriate response in a school, in a family, and in a community to foster healthy childhood development?

The answer to the last question is, of course, the purpose of this book. Once we thoroughly understand what precipitates the risk factors, we can more effectively and systematically formulate coherent, effective plans to reduce them. We can create community environments that produce healthy and resilient children who grow up to be capable, fully-functional adults.

Chapter 2

A Modern Social Experiment

A young person tends to be at greatest risk when he or she is experiencing too much stress and has inadequate resources to deal effectively with it. In this chapter, we will explore this increasing stress in the lives of our young people by examining the nature of societal change in the course of the last three generations.

What has led to the increased stress in the lives of children that has so severely undermined their development and ability to cope?

We can begin by looking at the changes in our society, primarily since World War II, in order to make sense of this perplexing phenomenon. However, before doing so, it is fitting to look at a simple model of childhood functioning as it occurs in a healthy environment, or what might be termed a healthy ecology for children. This healthy ecology is illustrated in Figure 3.

What we see are children surrounded by the four main or major institutions for child raising in the Western world. When these four institutions are, themselves, healthy and focused in a positive manner on the well-being of children, we enjoy a child-centered society. This implies that the main child-rearing elements

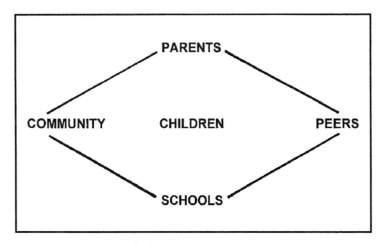

Figure 3. Healthy Ecology for Children

of a community or society consciously invest time, resources, and energy into the upcoming generation.

This investment assures a consistency in values transmission and real security for the aging generation. Jonas Salk said it best when he wrote, "children are the messages we send to a future that we shall never see."

This *healthy* ecology assures a safety net for children. It operated successfully for the vast majority during many, many generations. The emphasis, here, is on the word *healthy*, because we need not look too deeply into our major institutions to discover the sources of distress that young people today are mirroring.

As Dr. Bronfenbrenner points out, parents today are more stressed than at any time in the history of child rearing. Some statistics underscore what every parent knows in this regard, and emphasize the point about how this, in turn, stresses childhood. According to Richard Louv[3], writing in *Childhood's Future*, the amount of leisure time in America shrank from 26.2 hours per week in 1973, to 16.6 hours in 1987. He points to a Harris Poll which showed a thirty-seven percent drop in leisure— the time given over to relaxation, recreation, and family time.

George Gallup conducted a leisure poll in 1938 and reported the top three choices for leisure activities were: reading, movies, and dancing. Today, the top two are: T.V. and *resting*!

Louv cites two other findings which point to how much stress has entered our lives as parents and undermines our best efforts to raise healthy children.

According to the Family Research Council of Washington D.C., the amount of time parents spend with children has declined forty percent in the last twenty-five years. (In 1965, the average was thirty hours per week. Today's average is seventeen hours.) Between 1960 and 1986, the time parents have available to spend with their children decreased by 10 hours per week. This gives us a visceral sense of Dr. Bronfenbrenner's proclamation that it is the increasing *gulf* between significant adult figures and children that is directly responsible for the crisis in at-riskness today.

What is the result of these changes and stresses on parent-child relationships?

A study conducted by the Pittsburgh Priority Management Company in 1988 revealed that the average working couple spends about four minutes per day in meaningful conversation with each other, and only *thirty seconds* with their children. It comes as no great surprise, then, to discover that a Nickelodeon/Yankelovich Youth Monitor study in 1987 found the most sought-after thing in children's lives was more time with family.

These statistics underscore the concern we all feel about the increased stress occurring in life's most important relationship—parent to child. It needs to be stated, however, that we have always lived with stress. Parenting has always been a stressful business and life's exigencies have always challenged the resourcefulness of parents. What is markedly different today is, in addition to the subtle but dramatic decline in parent-child contact, we have the breakdown in connectedness in two other important child rearing institutions—community and school.

In the last forty years, our communities have become increasingly disorganized with respect to their roles in the child raising endeavor. Witness the virtual disappearance of apprenticeships and mentoring opportunities available to young persons, the lack of meaningful ritual to collectively celebrate transitions in and through childhood and adolescence, and the sluggishness that has occurred in response to a virtual crisis in providing good quality and affordable child care for working parents.

Then consider the situation that has developed in our schools over the last forty years. Since we will be looking in greater detail at these changes a bit later on, for now we can describe them in a word—depersonalization.

As this all-important adjunct to a healthy socialization of children responded to the demographic shifts and baby-boom of the 1940's and 1950's, it did so in a way that sacrificed personal contact. We shifted from a system of education to a system of schooling—and there is, as we shall see, an enormous difference between the two concepts in terms of childhood development.

In short, because of our collective ignorance of what was transpiring in these institutions, we awoke to discover a seemingly unbridgeable gulf between adults and children. We eventually looked about in dismay and horror at the results: tens of millions of at-risk young persons and an untold wreckage of millions of lives, undermining our society and our future.

The last institution providing the balance in the ecology of childhood is the peer group or network. It is interesting to view the changed nature of this element of childhood.

Take, as an example, the amount of time our grandparents spent interacting with their peers, as compared to young people today. Children today spend as much time in one day interacting with peers, free of adult supervision, as our grandparents would have spent in one month!

Thus, while parents, communities, and school have been unwittingly distancing themselves from the lives of children, and thereby broadening the gulf that creates risk, the peer institution has been playing an increasingly important, but questionable, role in child raising. The most exaggerated form and the most tragic is the proliferation of gangs, which serve as surrogate families for otherwise alienated youth.

In addition, there is the omnipresent and onerous influence of the media on the lives of children and teens. A mere fifty years ago, media was a minor player with young people. Today, driven by the advertising industry and the world's largest consumer society, it has become a major influence on our children's behaviors and values. Often, the values that are offered up for emulation by the media—conspicuous consumption, instant gratification, expedient violence, and gratuitous sex—are in direct and harmful contrast to that which best serves families, community and society. Yet by sheer force of numbers (parents interacting as little as thirty seconds per day with children and that same child interacting with the media for more than four hours per day), one can easily see which institution seems to have the upper hand in the all-important area of modeling values.

Having examined the general changes that have transpired in the ecology of children over that last forty years, let us turn to some specific changes in the two principal child-raising institutions since World War II—family and school.

What follows is more or less a synopsis of the work of H. Stephen Glenn[4], who so clearly explains the impact of societal change on childraising in the last forty to fifty years.

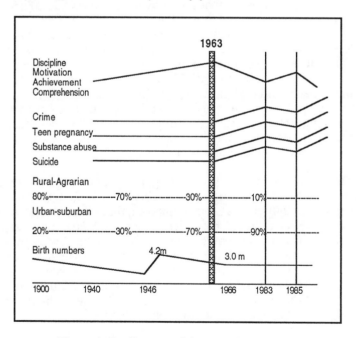

Figure 4: Predictors and demographic changes
Source: H. Stephen Glenn, Raising Self-Reliant Children
in a Self-indulgent World, *Sunrise Press.*

In the graphic in Figure 4, we note a growing improvement in some predictors of positive outcomes among young people, between 1900 and 1963. These predictors include discipline, motivation, achievement, and comprehension. That is to say, with each passing graduation class or generation, things seem to have gotten better in terms of young people's ability to capably step into an adult world as competent, relatively integrated adult figures.

Below that we see measures of problem behaviors—crime, teen pregnancy, substance abuse and suicide. In these areas, we see a relatively constant number of problems all the way across to 1963. After 1963, the picture changes.

All indicators show that every graduating class since 1963 was somehow doing worse in every area (whether it was college tests, ability to comprehend, or competitive international scores.) They continue to do worse and worse for about twenty years. There was a brief upturn for about three years in the middle-80's followed by a steeper downturn than we have ever seen. That downturn continues while the problem behaviors of our young tend to rise. We get this interesting mirror-like situation. The only outstanding example to the contrary is drug abuse, which, overall, has gone down since 1983. (We should note, however, that tobacco and alcohol abuse remain at record levels with our young, and those are the two most dangerous drugs our kids are using. If we were to successfully eliminate all the other drugs we would still have an epidemic of alcohol and tobacco use which are two major killers in this country.)

The experts who were invited to participate in a presidential study of these escalating problems began to explore these dynamics. Eventually, as Glenn points out, they isolated two critical factors relating to *all* those changes and problems. Both were related to changing demographics. One was the shift from an agrarian, rural population to more of a suburban/urban lifestyle. At the turn of the century, eighty percent of Americans were farmers or otherwise associated with a rural, agrarian lifestyle. Contrast that, if you will, with today's society where ninety percent of us are part of an urban/suburban population.

The second was the increased birthrate or "baby boom" that occurred following World War II.

So what is the significance of these two changes as they relate to the escalating problems of our young children?

The table in Figure 5 presents a series of lifestyle norms as they existed fifty to sixty years ago and as they exist today. Obviously, things have changed a great deal in a relatively short time frame.

Major Transitions in Life-style

Characteristics	Norm 1930	Norm 1980
Family interaction	high	low
Value System	homogenous	heterogenous
Role models	consonant	dissonant
Logical consequences	experienced	avoided
Inter-general associations	many	few
Education	less	more
Level of information	low	high
Technology	low	high
Non-negotiable tasks	many	few
Family work	much	little
Family size	large	small
Family dominant	extended	nuclear
Single-parent/blended/step families	few (10% - 15%)	many (35%-42%)
Class size (K - 12)	18-22	28-35
Neighborhood schools	dominant	rare

Figure 5: Norms for the 1930's and 1980's
Source: H. Stephen Glenn, Raising Self-Reliant Children
in a Self-indulgent World, *Sunrise Press.*

Perhaps the most significant factor related to risk is the altered pattern of family relationships. To more fully appreciate this change, let us consider the broadest possible historical perspective in child-rearing.

Family Life Then and Now

For the 50,000 years of social history studied by anthropologists—all the way up to the industrial revolution—there was a remarkable similarity in the way children were raised. A child was raised by parents in what we might call a traditional or nuclear family which was embedded completely within an extended family. Living under the same roof, would often times be grandparents, aunts and uncles, and other, more distant, relatives. A child had the benefit of a nuclear and extended family in a kinship system. Blood relatives were always close by.

> *When children were raised by the village, there were adequate safety nets for them as well as natural relationships, apprenticeships, and other means of obtaining on-the-job training for life. For 50,000 years, we did this successfully—until the industrialization and agrarian mechanization of World War II transformed us into a society where we raise our children in the cities and suburbs.*

Furthermore, each family was supported in the context of the community or tribe, giving rise to the African proverb, "It takes a whole village to raise a child." When children were raised by the village, there were adequate safety nets for them as well as natural relationships, apprenticeships, and other means of obtaining on-the-job training for life. For 50,000 years, we did this successfully—until the industrialization and agrarian mechanization of World War II transformed us into a society where we raise our children in the cities and suburbs. At that point, we embarked on what social anthropologists call the greatest experiment in child raising in 50,000 years: the nuclear family. The results, by and large, can be seen in Figure 5, beginning in 1963.

Glenn underscores the fact that our relationship patterns shifted because of social changes that accompanied the end of World War II. Five and one-half million G.I.s returned from the war. They and their wives perceived a new dream—a dream of material abundance and material fulfillment. Largely as a direct result of World War II, farming had become more and more mechanized, requiring less human labor. Because work was in the cities and suburbs, eleven million people pulled up stakes and moved in one of the largest intra-national migrations in world history. This was among the most significant social migrations in history, and with it began one of the biggest social experiments in child-raising the world has ever known.

Again, this social experiment can best be understood by looking more closely at the changed pattern of societal and family norms, illustrated in Figure 5.

The average family in the 1930s spent three to four hours each day with members interacting in a way that reflected the meaning of their daily lives and daily experiences. Generally, much of it happened in the biggest room of the house, which was usually the kitchen. Most kitchens were large rooms with big tables around which most family interactions occurred. In his book, *Raising Self-reliant Children in a Self-indulgent World*, Glenn indicates that in middle-class families today, the amount of time that a father spends interacting with his child on a given day is about twelve and one-half *minutes*. Furthermore, most of that twelve and one-half minutes is taken up with interactions that actually suppress maturity and suppress learning, such as correcting, advising, controlling, lecturing, and explaining.

Glenn points out that a more beneficial interaction would be that of spending time helping the child explore and understand the meaning of experiences through the father's encouragement and support. This scenario, of course, assumes that the father is around at all. Various demographic studies indicate that the normative experience in this society will soon be the presence of only a part-time father because of separation, divorce and so forth.

That is to say that of children born since 1980, sixty percent will have been raised, at least part of the time, by a single parent.

When interaction and dialogue are measurably reduced between significant others, and substituted with increased exposure to media and peers, we have a perfect prescription for risk. Once again, when considering the fact that the average child spends as much time with peers in a day as her great-grandparents would have spent in a month, and spends literally hours each day passively absorbing media messages and values, is it really any wonder that we are having such an unprecedented crisis?

Classroom Interactions

Next we look at changes in schools. The typical school in 1930 was small with classes made up of a mixture of older and younger students. Those varying age groups, sharing a small classroom, allowed older and younger children to connect and to bond. Younger children got the bonding and access to older role models that they needed while older youngsters developed a sense of meaning and significance in their lives through the act of contributing to their juniors. Today's norm is large schools with many students in crowded classrooms.

How did our schools change to meet the impact of all these children being born? They introduced age stratification as we doubled and even tripled the size of the class. For the first time in history, we used an industrial, mass-model of schooling for a large population. In the process we removed the younger children's access to positive role-models and prevented older children from getting a sense of meaning and accomplishment by working with the younger students. We removed the opportunity for the older ones to role model, to tutor, and to teach useful skills to others.

In a word, we removed a significant avenue for developing a strong sense of meaning in life by removing the opportunity to *contribute*, completely undermining the natural ecology in education that had been used for generations.

Thus it was that we put children in a passive learning mode for six to eight hours each day, in large classrooms with limited access to older, mature role-models. The teacher became more active, with the students learning passively. Then they went home and spent an average of three to four hours each day passively watching television. This further reduced not only the opportunity for interacting with positive role-models, but also the opportunity in such an environment for meaningful bonding.

In that atmosphere, we go from 1951, when the first baby-boomers entered school, to 1963, when they started graduating. In 1963, we start seeing a marked decline in discipline, motivation, and achievement while crime, teen pregnancy, substance abuse and suicide increase. Overall, this trend worsened, prompting President Carter to bring a group of experts (including Stephen Glenn) together to look at the data and draw conclusions. What they eventually decided was that the tactics that we tried in the 60's and 70's to turn this around used the wrong set of assumptions.

We assumed that if we looked at all these symptoms—teen pregnancy, suicide, runaways, alcohol/drug abuse, low self-esteem and so forth, and we put our time, energy and money into programs and agencies which could effectively rehabilitate our youngsters, we could get back on track. We did that all through the '60s and '70s but things continued to get worse.

New Assumptions for Action

We finally realized that we can't assume young people can be _re_habilitated, as Glenn points out, if they have never been _habilitated_ in the first place. If we are raising children in our families, schools, and communities who don't have basic habilitation skills—coping skills or skills for living life successfully—it is not going to do any good to try to _rehabilitate_ them. We have got to habilitate them first—and the only way that can happen is when families, schools, and communities consistently work well together, much as villages used to do. Unfortunately, we haven't done that very successfully for the last two generations.

The results of that failure are graphic in terms of the number of problems. Not only do we have a million teen pregnancies, but every day, forty teenagers give birth _to their third child_ in America. Suicide and depression are at record levels—considered epidemic, by some. Sixty percent of our 7th to 12th grade children use alcohol weekly, and so on.

For years, we attempted to bring the bottom set of lines—the problems—down. We set up discrete agencies and programs to deal with teen pregnancy, substance abuse, suicide, runaway children, and drop out prevention. We used a model of rehabilitation (tertiary prevention) that is, basically, "treatment." The problem was that the results were fairly dismal. For example, only about 15 percent of young people who complete treatment for chemical dependency remain chemical free for more than a year. Eventually, it began to dawn on us that our assumptions

> *Instead of having brothers and sisters, aunts, uncles, and grandparents around the household to work beside, bond with, communicate with, and share experiences with, we put our kids in front of the TV and unwittingly expose them to the influences of negative role-models that TV provides.*

were ill-founded. At that point, our attention turned to the upper portion of the graph, and the possibility that, maybe, we should focus more on the *assets* that create capability instead of the risk behaviors. In doing so, three factors related to the decline in capability eventually emerged.

First: it was determined that the major sociological change affecting families, schools, and communities was that young people were experiencing less and less access to positive role-models. They had less time to spend with older, mature adults who could mentor and guide them and they had fewer opportunities to participate and contribute. The result was a steep decline in young people's perception that their lives were meaningful, significant, and connected to the larger community.

That made sense. If one of life's greatest needs, as Glenn says, is to have a sense of meaning, and meaning begins to disintegrate, we are going to have problems in our lives. If I am a 15-year old female and I don't have a strong sense of meaning, significance, purpose and belonging in my family, school or community, why wouldn't sex provide at least a momentary sense that I am needed and appreciated? If I am a 14-year old boy who doesn't have a sense of meaning, purpose, significance, and belonging in my family, school or community, why shouldn't I use drugs? Drugs will make me feel good for a little while. What about joining a gang? A gang provides a sense of identity, meaning and belonging, however harmful and destructive.

Second: it was obvious that we were suffering from an increase in alcohol consumption and other drug abuse. It doesn't take a big stretch to understand how alcohol and drugs can be attractive to young people who are emotionally adrift. It is a most insidious situation because the prolonged use of alcohol and drugs literally can disrupt and even destroy one's sense of meaning, purpose, significance, and belonging.

Third: there is an increased exposure to *negative* social role-models rather than positive. When we took away the older siblings and older peers by age-stratifying our classrooms, the opportunity for children to have close proximity to positive role-models began to disappear. We also took away the opportunity for the older children to work with adults while contributing to the community. Instead of having brothers and sisters, aunts, uncles, and grandparents around the household to work beside, bond with, communicate with, and share experiences with, we put our kids in front of the TV and unwittingly expose them to the influences of negative role-models that TV provides.

In summation, we are now more aware that is was the *disappearance* of elements of our family, school, and community life—factors that had existed for generations—that was the source of our problems. Less time spent in the presence of positive role models, more time in the negative influences, fewer opportunities to be involved and challenged in meaningful ways, fewer opportunities to contribute to the well-being of others, less bonding and connectedness, and greater access to alcohol and other drugs—all would add up to our present-day crisis.

Overall, the net effect of increased affluence, mobility, and heterogeneity was to widen the gulf between adults and children. This, in turn, has increased the level of alienation and meaninglessness in many of today's young people. This alienation and meaninglessness was further exacerbated by and resulted from the problems related to childhood development imperatives that were going unmet on a large scale. It is the topic of childhood development to which we now turn.

Chapter 3:
Developmental
Needs in Childhood

Having covered the external or social ramifications of risk in our social environment, we turn to the other side of the formulation of "at-risk" young people having to do with unmet developmental needs—the inner ramifications. To do this, we will look at the inner world of the child. In an earlier book, *Our Children, Our Future*, I went into a great deal of detail about developmental factors associated with risk that have to do with brain development and learning. Instead of presenting this information in detail here, I want to highlight a few factors having to do with childhood development, from a slightly different angle.

These factors relate to essential elements in any view of healthy childhood development, and play a key role in providing a base for resilience and the ability to overcome adversity.

One factor is the role of self-concept and its antecedents: self-worth and self-esteem. Another factor is the nature of human bonding and how that relates to spirituality. A third factor is the nature of learning as it interfaces with bonding and spirituality. In addition, we will examine the importance of modeling in the learning and development process.

Nancy Phillips and Self-Concept

In writing about childhood development and its relationship to eventual risk behaviors, Nancy Phillips[5] provides an interesting and important perspective (also, please see Appendix D). In particular, Phillips was interested in what, if any, overarching factor could serve to prevent risk behaviors as children move into the teen years. She proposes that there does exist just such a factor: a healthy, positive self-concept.

Phillips, of course, is not alone in her assertion. Over the years, any number of observers have described the importance of positive self-concept to overall well being in life.

In the graphic below, we see the three most basic human needs—bonding, meaning, and control—and the way in which they interrelate to create a strong, positive self-concept, according to Phillips.

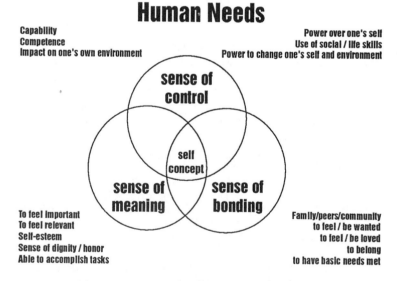

Source: Nancy Phillips, "Wellness During Childhood / Adolescent Development", Prevention Forum, Vol. 10, Issue 4, July 1990

Figure 6: Human Needs and Self-concept

When a young person enjoys a strong, positive self-concept, that young person usually enjoys a very low-risk behavior pattern[6]. Self-concept derives from a sense of control, a sense of meaning, and a sense of bonding.

A sense of control can be understood as the central need of a young person for power to influence the forces that shape him or her. It is the conviction that a young person is participating in an interactive process and exerting some direct control over what is happening in his or her life.

A sense of bonding means a sense of belonging. A young person must feel a part of the major institutions that comprise his or her environment—family, school, and community. Its opposite is, of course, alienation.

A sense of meaning is a young person's belief that he or she is significant and important. It is the experience of congruence and coherence derived from the pattern of experiences in life.

The youngster who plays a meaningful part in the life of the family, school, and community, who exercises the self-discipline necessary to exert reasonable control over his or her environment, and perceives the order inherent in life develops a healthy, strong, positive self-concept.

The Developing Self

Nancy Phillips provides a meaningful framework and starting point for an inquiry into the nature of self-development. Positive self-concept is inextricably connected to well-being in adolescence. Self-concept, in fact, has often been understood as a "self-fulfilling prophecy." By this, we mean that if I see myself as competent and capable, I will usually act as such, experiencing results and successes that reinforce my concept of self. Conversely, if I view myself as a failure, it is more than likely that my actions will produce unsuccessful outcomes, thus reinforcing a negative self-concept.

What, then, are the antecedents of self-concept? What determines the degree to which a child achieves a strong sense of control, bonding, and meaning?

From a developmental perspective, we can look at how the growing self takes shape. There are at least four major, somewhat sequential, forces or factors that help to shape our self-concept.

Self-Worth

Child development experts tell us that self-worth is a foundational factor in a child's life. It has to do with love that is received and trust that is generated. Self-worth appears to be largely established around age two. That is not to say that a child's self-worth is totally set in concrete at such a young age. It can still be changed and influenced. However, it is a little harder to develop a sense of self-worth as one gets older, because self-worth comes from the loving contact and trust experienced in one's earliest, and most vulnerable years of life—infancy.

Self-worth is an integral part of my human "beingness" and yours. It is the result of the amount of love, respect, and tenderness that was received just for being—what we often call *unconditional love*. It has nothing to do with what is accomplished or what is done. It is love that is given simply because we exist within a caring community. Figure 7 illustrates the critical position that self-worth occupies in human development. It is the foundation of the self.

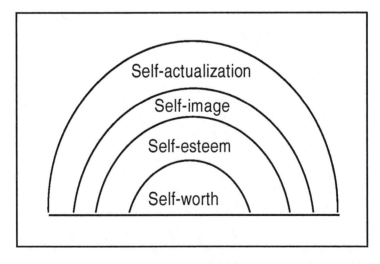

Figure 7: Development of Self-concept

Self-esteem

Growing directly out of self-worth is self-esteem. Although these words are sometimes used interchangeably, self-esteem, in my estimation, is an outgrowth of human "doingness." My self-esteem is the result of my successes, my accomplishments and my achievements. It varies from situation to situation. My personal self-esteem as a teacher, an instructor, a trainer, and a workshop leader, on a scale of one to one-hundred, is probably close to one-hundred all the time. My self-esteem as an automobile mechanic varies between zero and ten almost all the time. I don't have much self-esteem in that area at all. Why not? Because I haven't spent much time accomplishing, achieving and doing in that area. In this definition, self-esteem is variable and situational.

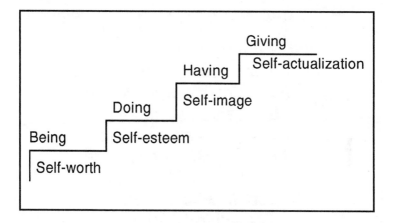

Figure 8: Self-esteem

What allows a person, to develop more self-esteem in new areas is the degree to which he or she can draw from a reservoir of *self-worth* and take the risk of trying something new—even in the face of possible failure. Anyone entering into a new situation, faces some likelihood of failure. But *everything* at which we succeeded took practice. There were probably multiple failures before you and I mastered any skill or task. Think of something you are good at: cooking, sewing, a sport or a musical instrument. Do you and remember how many times you had to practice and try before you became proficient at it? None of us is a "natural" at all skills and endeavors.

What kept us going in spite of the early failures was the sense of self-worth or self-love that we developed prior to age two. It's the belief that "I'm OK." People are able to accept and learn from failure when they love and accept themselves. Thomas Edison said it most succinctly: "Many, many failures equals success."

It follows then, that if we are really interested in boosting children's self-esteem, we need to provide them environments with many loving and supportive learning opportunities. After age two, when children are starting to do things on their own initiative, they need to be placed in situations where they can explore, risk and make mistakes as they learn and succeed. From that type of experience, successes occur and self-esteem is generated.

> *It is hardly surprising that an enormous portion of the country's advertising budgets are aimed at young people whose self-images are in the formative stage. These are people who are most easily influenced.*

Self-Image

There is another aspect of the self related to *self-image*. Self-image has to do, in part, with how I view my self—my body in particular. It also has to do with how I think others think about me or perceive me. In today's society, a person's self-image is increasingly being manipulated by the media, which is one of the most subtle, yet powerful, features of our day-to-day experience. It is absolutely pervasive. For most Americans, it is almost impossible to escape the influence of television and radio, magazine and newspaper advertising. So in this media-saturated environment, we are continually being influenced by the image makers. Madison Avenue spends billions of dollars to impact and influence our buying decisions on everything from clothes to music and movies; from food and beverages to cars and homes, vitamins and face tissues. The basis of all advertising campaigns is to impact and influence the self-image of the potential customer. The not-so-subtle message is that buying their product makes a person more beautiful, desirable, or powerful and important. Those who are most vulnerable to these messages are most certainly those with the least sense of worth or esteem; that is, little sense of self.

It is hardly surprising that an enormous portion of the country's advertising budgets are aimed at young people whose self-images are in the formative stage. These are people who are most easily influenced. It is interesting to note that the young people who seem most resistant to peer and media influences, are those who have high self-esteem and positive self-worth. In other words, their self-image is well-guarded and less vulnerable. On the other hand, a youngster who is low in self-worth and who doesn't have a lot of self-esteem in different areas is more likely to be overly concerned about self-image. He or she is a prime target for media influences. In extreme cases, these children are capable of doing mind-boggling things. It is no longer unusual to read about one teenager who murders another in order to steal his designer sports shoes or special jacket. These are young people whose lack of a positive self-image leads them to believe that the mere acquisition of a prestige item of clothing will make them feel powerful, important, and loved.

Self-Actualization: The Sum of the Selves

After self-image comes *self-actualization*. We reach a state of self-actualization when we begin to use our lives to give something back to our families, our community, and our world. This usually happens naturally when enough of our self-needs have been met. Self-actualization, then, is a natural outgrowth of the very human desire to serve, contribute, and provide for the well-being of others. These are, I believe, innate drives in all of us.

Self-worth, self-esteem, self-image, and self-actualization, then, are all part of the self-concept. Self-concept is the totality of my beliefs about my strengths and weaknesses, and my judgments about myself—for good or for bad, for better or for worse.

Self-concept is the keystone determining whether or not young people are "at-risk". In order to help bolster and build self-concept, we must provide arenas in which children can feel powerful and in control of their lives. We have to foster a sense of meaning and purpose, and help provide them with a sense of belonging.

Self-concept, not surprisingly, lies at the heart of resilience.

Bonding: The spiritual base of childhood

When Stephen Glenn refers to the rapid decline of such positive indicators of youth development as self-discipline, achievement, and motivation, he points out that it represents the spiritual decline of a society. What is spirituality? How does it develop in childhood (or fail to develop)? What is the relationship of spirituality to human and societal potential?

To begin with, we need look no farther than the word *psychology* to begin establishing the important place of spirituality in the life and development of a human being. The word derives from the Greek *psyche*, which means spirit. Psychology is the study of spirit or spirituality in human terms. In modern times, however, it has rarely even acknowledged spirituality, let alone helped us to clarify or deal with it.

Let us look at the table in Figure 9, taken from my earlier book, *Our Children, Our Future*. It is an attempt to synthesize a good deal of information about childhood development.

Included in this figure, are stages of brain growth and development, levels of intelligence, some of the key issues that come into play at each level, and how they relate to the work of five developmental theorists. For this portion, I selected Jean Piaget, who was interested in the cognitive development of humans, Eric Erickson who was primarily interested in social and emotional development, Abraham Maslow, who looked at the hierarchy of human needs, Lawrence Kohlberg who focused on moral development in children, and, finally, Rudolph Steiner who studied what we might call spiritual development in children.

Developmental Stages

Brain Development Stage and Age	Level of Intelligence & Key Issue	Theorist: Piaget (Cognitive)	Theorist: Erikson (Soc/Emotional)	Theorist: Maslow (Need hierarchy)	Theorist: Kohlberg (Moral)	Theorist: Steiner (Spiritual)
Reptilian (brain-stem) Birth to 2 yrs	1. Physical: Self-preservation & survival	Sensorimotor	Trust vs mistrust	Survival, safety, and satisfaction		Goodness orientation
Paleomammalian (limbic cortex) 2 to 6 yrs.	2. Emotional: relationship	Preoperational	Autonomy vs shame	Love and affection orientation	Punishment and obedience	Beauty orientation
Neomammalian A. Posterior Cortex 6-12 or 13 yrs.	3. Thought: Concrete thinking & problem solving.	Concrete operational	Initiative vs guilt / Industry vs inferiority	Belongingness orientation	Instrumental operational / Interpersonal concordance	Truth orientation
Neomammalian B. Frontal Cortex teens to adult	4. Thought: Abstract thinking & meaning making.	Formal operational	Identity vs identity diffusion	Esteem & esteem orientation	Social orientation	Soul orientation
Mind-heart connection	5. Heart: Compassion & service	—	Intimacy vs isolation	Self-actualization	Principled orientation	Possible spiritual orientation

Figure 9: Brain Development Stages

This is basically a map of how some theorists look at the stages of childhood development. Because the foundation of human development is self-worth, we can use this chart to determine that the corollary of self-worth, during the first two years of life, is the degree to which a child achieves or receives sufficient love, bonding, trust and safety in his/her relationships. Erickson talked about this in terms of the polar opposites of trust and distrust, which is another way of describing bonding and abandonment.

To the degree to which our children experience bonding with an emotionally invested care-giver (a nurturing parent, relative or other consistent, emotionally involved care-giver), there will be the development of a sense of trust. If we look across the chart at the basic issues of those first two years of life, as a child is developing self-worth, the amount of bonding and love in the environment is the critical issue. This is all happening at a time that precedes recall . (Not many of us can remember anything prior to the age of two.) It is largely going to precede language development, so the child is going to receive messages about trusting and goodness mostly through the close proximity of loving people and in the physical and emotional relationships with those people.

Steiner, the brilliant, turn-of-the-century German scientist, artist, and guiding force behind the Waldorf School movement, said that the most important thing in early childhood, is the sense of *goodness*. He believed that a child needs to experience the world as a good place, as a necessary condition to the development of connectedness and spirit in a child. (It is interesting to note that the word religion comes from the Latin *religio*, which means to re-connect. To connect, of course, is to bond.)

Self-worth, then, is derived from feelings of safety, security, trust, love, and goodness. It is primarily a spiritual process—an immaterial transmission of energy, love, and goodness to the growing child's being.

When Joseph Chilton Pearce[7], brilliant thinker and author of many fine books on childhood, examined childhood development, he came to the conclusion that *unconditional love and acceptance is the major criteria for the development of intelligence.* His writings breathe profound life into that conclusion.

Human intelligence, which is related to the biological development of the brain, can only unfold in an atmosphere of unconditional love and acceptance. Pearce goes to great lengths to explain how the structure of intelligence undergoes fundamental changes when it is repeatedly faced with the threat of abandonment or harm. If there is too much threat in the environment, the structure of intelligence becomes defensive, controlling, and closed. It cannot unfold. After all, if my survival is at stake, I am going to pull in and defend myself at all costs.

To the extent the child is raised or schooled in a community where there is constant threat of any type, be it violence or abandonment, the structure of defensiveness develops more and more strongly. The longer he stays in a defensive posture, the more controlling he becomes with his life. The focus is on controlling feelings, thoughts, and potential threats, rather than exploring and cooperating, which are both natural to children and conducive to the development of intelligence. Where there is a perception of safety and security, the child can feel comfortable about being open to life, thereby promoting the development of intelligence, characterized by openness, inquisitiveness, cooperation and creativity.

Intellect versus Intelligence

Intellect, Pearce says, asks only, "Is it *possible?*" and then goes about solving the problem at hand. This quality of intellect can be measured with a test and given a number, or intelligence quotient (I.Q.) In its classic form, intellect removes an element from its total environment, manipulates and alters it, then puts it back into the whole. An example is Pearce's description of chemists who are involved in the development and manufacture of chemicals so toxic that no known container can safely store them for any length of time. Annually, over 9,000 such chemicals compounds have been developed. This unthinking disregard for the whole picture—in this case the environmental consequences—is, Pearce instructs us, *intellect* at work.

Intelligence, on the other hand, always asks, "Is it *appropriate?*" Intelligence, therefore, is concerned with the big picture, the overall well being of all and everything concerned, and always includes an element of heart—understanding combined with compassion and sensitivity to the whole of a situation. This overall concern for the well-being of the whole takes us back to the notion of spirituality. In the same way that the word *religion* connotes a reconnection or rebonding with something greater than ourselves, so too does the word *spirituality*.

So let us attempt to define spirituality. I like Stephen Glenn's definition: "Spirituality is an active sense of identification with a power greater than self which gives our lives a sense of meaning, significance, and purpose." To say that spirituality is an active sense of identification is another way of saying that there is *involvement.*

Whatever I am identified with, I am involved in. This involvement, when it is based on respect, care, and concern, fosters intelligence. The active identification, as I involve myself in it, becomes part of me. As I become identified with an idea, or if I become identified with a role-model, that role-model or idea becomes part of me—it becomes part of who I am developmentally.

To be bonded or connected is to become actively involved in the life-force of another. This life-force is, quite simply, love itself.

> **When we are involved with a power greater than ourselves, that power gives our lives a sense of meaning, significance, and purpose. This definition helps us to understand otherwise unfathomable occurrences such as why young people join gangs.**

Philosophers and sages of every age considered love the most powerful force in the universe. In his book, *The Road Less Traveled*[8], author Scott Peck defines love as the commitment one has to the spiritual development and growth of another. The research synthesized by Pearce clearly indicates to us that love plays *the* central role in learning and intelligence.

The brain is designed to seek out a model to follow. That model eventually becomes part of who we are. After all, none of us would be able to speak any language that we use for communication if not for the presence of a model. The model never "taught" us how to talk. We learned to talk because we were in the presence of the model and we were involved with that model. Most of us are familiar, for example, with stories of children who, because they were raised in isolation and were never spoken to, were later unable to learn speech.

When we are involved with a power greater than ourselves, that power gives our lives a sense of meaning, significance, and purpose. This definition helps us to understand otherwise unfathomable occurrences such as why young people join gangs. It helps us understand why all those people followed James Jones to Guyana and committed mass suicide. Although the outcome is often quite horrible, joining a gang, getting involved in fascism, or becoming attached to a figure like David Koresh is a search for a higher meaning and a sense of purpose and belonging. It is a spiritual quest.

Nature's First Mandate for Development

Evidently, then, a basic human drive is to connect with a power greater than ourselves. I think that is why people can bond with good or evil, because they are responding to a biological, most probably genetic, and certainly emotional imperative. Pearce, in fact, says bonding is the first great biological imperative of human beings.

Who or what is that power greater than self that shapes the belonging, the purpose, and the significance of a child in the period between birth and age two? Most of the time, it is Mother.

Let's make no mistake. When that child is in a relationship with mom, by this definition, that is a spiritual experience. It is a powerful, physical experience for a human being entailing touch, caressing, and close physical proximity. At this stage, God is, literally, mother or nurturing father, or nurturing aunt or grandparent. The basic requirement for proper development of the human being is enough emotional attention by a care-giver who is genuinely involved with the child.

If we track the development of a human being through all five stages listed on the chart, we notice that the nature of the bond of spirituality changes in each stage. As a child grows from the dominance of the reptilian brain through the limbic brain (that is the emotional-relational brain), we have a child involved in mastery of emotional development during the preschool years (age two to six). Who or what is the higher power that is going to shape the child during this emotional relationship stage of life? It is *family*. The child goes from a one-to-one relationship, which is spiritual in every sense of the word, to a period in which that child increasingly expands his or her field of relationships to family members. The family is the major determinant of the child's spiritual development and potential at that point.

What tasks are being mastered in the pre-school years? During infancy, the child forms his or her basic concepts of the world, along with a strong sense of bonding, trust, and worthiness. The next stage, lasting from infancy until the start of school at age six, lays the foundation for emotional and relationship mastery.

Nature's Second Mandate for Development

According to Pearce, the driving force that emerges at this point in childhood is the need to overcome obstacles to development. That is the purpose behind the emergence of will. The power of will as it develops in a two or three year-old is non-volitional—out of the child's control. It finds its most common expression in the toddler's frequent use of the word, "No!" This is perhaps the purest and clearest outpouring of will-power that can be seen in someone so young. I find it terribly ironic that, as a society we recently had to invent an entire governmentally-initiated program to teach kids to, "Just Say No." If, as a people, we understood, appreciated, and supported our children's developmental mandates a little better, perhaps far fewer of them would be so vulnerable to a variety of pressures as teenagers.

Taken together, these two apparently biologically and genetically derived drives create a firm foundation for proper development in childhood. Bonding, experienced as love and support, is followed by opportunities to face and overcome challenges, expressed as learning, exploration, and participation in life. Both stand as the foundation from which all further development ensues. Bonding provides self-worth or self-love while facing challenges successfully builds self-esteem. These are the definitive and distinctive "bottom-line" for healthy development. They form, albeit in different language, the key constructs of childhood resilience, as we shall see.

Given this background, let's look more closely at the nature of learning. The brain of a human being is—first, foremost, and forever—an organ for learning. We are uniquely endowed with an ability to learn throughout our entire life span, and this could legitimately be considered the third mandate of nature: learn!

Nature's Third Mandate for Development

The brain, it has been shown, has an irrepressible need to learn and becomes bored and distractible in the absence of new challenges and opportunities to learn. For new learning to take place, and for intelligence to unfold, nature seems to have three requirements:

- Modeling

- Mirroring

- Support and Encouragement

Modeling

First and foremost, is modeling. Why is modeling the most important? Because ninety to ninety-five percent of all human learning is based on relationships to and involvement with a person. That person can be either real or imaginary, where an imaginary model is an historical figure or a fictional character. Only five to ten percent of what we learn is what we call prescribed learning, or learning from explicit directions. "Do this." "Don't do that."

47

Modeled learning is largely unconscious. It is picking up on nonverbal cues, tone of voice, and what is in the environment. It is based upon the quality of the relationship. So if ninety to ninety-five percent of all learning is modeled learning, it means that we need to focus on *ourselves* as models; the kind of life we are living and the example we set. This is a theme to which we will be returning in the last section of the book As the saying goes, "We teach a louder sermon with our lives than we do with our lips."

The great early 20th century poet, Edgar Guest expressed the same idea in a different way in his poem called *The Living Sermon*.

> I'd rather see a sermon, than to hear one any day.
>
> I'd rather one should walk with me than to merely show the way.
>
> I can soon learn how to do it, if you'd let me see it done.
>
> I can watch your hands in action but your tongue too fast may run.
>
> All the lectures you deliver may be very wise and true,
>
> But I'd rather get my lesson by observing what you do.
>
> Though I might not understand you and the fine advice you give.
>
> There's no misunderstanding how you act and how you live.

If we want to build resiliency in our children, we are challenged by the awareness that it is who we are, so much more than what we say, that makes the difference in providing that essential life ingredient. What children never miss and never fail to learn from is what they see in the environment—the actions and attitudes of the people who are, for better or worse, models. In this respect, modeled learning becomes the prime factor in the emotional and spiritual development (and all other aspects of learning) of our children.

Mirroring

A second aspect involved in learning is mirroring. Mirroring takes place from infancy on. Observing ourselves or another holding an infant, we are often witness to the naturalness of

> *For busy parents, especially when both are working, it is important to help with this critical process [mirroring] whenever possible by watching and listening, then reflecting children's experiences back to them.*

mirroring. Both the adult and the infant are frequently engaged in mirroring facial expressions and sounds which go back and forth. There is an instinctive need to interact with the baby, it seems. We make faces and the baby makes faces back. This activity is actually helping the brain of that infant to develop and it is certainly one aspect of bonding.

For the child who is no longer an infant, parental mirroring changes. Mirroring now means taking the *time* to be a mirror for that child while he/she learns emotional mastery and learns about relationships. What it means is taking the time to be at the child's emotional level—to give the child what he or she needs in terms of working through problems, relationships, and emotions. What it entails is providing time, attention and feedback. It is the words we use to teach, as well as our empathetic understanding of the child's experience.

Mirroring has to do with taking the time to help our children process and understand new experiences. What concerns all of us is that we seem to have less and less time for our children at this critical stage. It takes time to help children learn from their experiences. For busy parents, especially when both are working, it is important to help with this critical process whenever possible by watching and listening, then reflecting children's experiences back to them.

Support and Encouragement

The third component of all learning is the contextual element. It is love expressed as support and encouragement. With it, children can overcome almost any adversity and obstacle to development. Without support and encouragement, their ability to learn, grow in intelligence, and bounce back from adversity is curtailed.

There is one final point to be made about modeling. It comes from research on the unique role of modeling in learning. According to Pearce, research conducted at Harvard University Center for Cognitive Studies has been undertaken to look at what is called the "cycle of competence," which could also be called the "cycle of learning." How does one move from incompetence to competence? How does one move from not knowing and uncertainty to a state of mastery?

In answer to these important questions, the Harvard researchers propose a three step process:

- Stimulus of a Model

- Practice, Repetition, and Variation

- Application

Step #1: In any new learning, the first step on the road to competency and mastery is the stimulus of modeling. In every case, a model is required to stimulate new learning. This, for our purposes, further validates the singular importance of the role of modeling.

Step #2: After coming into contact with some modeled behavior, there must be opportunities for practice. Any new behavior we learn requires the stimulus of a model followed by an opportunity to practice and improve upon the behavior. This often requires repetition and variation as well.

Step #3: This is what distinguishes human learning from animal learning. All animals require a relationship with a model and frequent practice to learn new behaviors. Only humans seem fully capable of transferring or generalizing prior learning to new and novel circumstances.

Aikido is a good example of this creative learning cycle, or cycle of competence, and one that utilizes the fact that ninety-five percent of all learning is modeled (and, therefore largely unconscious.) *Aikido* is a martial art, perhaps the only one that emphasizes entirely defensive forms. It accomplishes that goal with a distinctive teaching style, remarkable in at least one respect for the minimal role of talking. Most practice sessions emphasize the instructor's thorough demonstration of a technique. This is the stimulus of a model. Students watch carefully and then proceed to repeat and practice the movements as close to the instructor's modeling as possible.

Most correction occurs through further demonstration and directed practice with the instructor. Finally, application of the principles and methods of *aikido* are not limited to self-defense situations, but eventually begin to apply more broadly to areas of life where there is a need to deal effectively with conflict of any type.

Access to the model, practice, variation,, and application, form the interactional context by which human learning takes place. What are the internal correlates or changes that coincide with this broad basis for learning? In other words, to what degree does new learning impact and change the brain? Finally, what can these brain changes—for better of worse—teach us about well-being and human resilience? It is to these important questions that we turn in the final chapter of this section.

Chapter 4: The Neurophysiology of Learning

The major activity of the brain is to learn. It is, very simply, an organ for learning.

Learning is the activity by which we relate our experiences in a patterned and connected way. The goal of all learning is first survival, and then, "thrival," by which I mean achieving a *quality* life. Life that is marked by increased awareness, sensitivity, wisdom, creativity, and service is life well lived, in my view.

At a time when our society increasingly accepts what seems to be a reduction in functioning in those areas, we find ourselves witnessing a greater insensitivity, ignorance, and destruction. In the words of Dr. Jane Healy, "What we do with, for, and to our children's growing minds will shape not only their brains but also the standards that represent our cultural future."[9]

Benefits can be derived from examining brain functioning as it relates to learning, since the nature of one's experience greatly alters the way one's brain functions and responds to the world.

Neurons and Synapses

What is actually occurring in the brain, when learning takes place? To understand this, we need to examine the neural level of brain function. The brain contains some 10 billion specialized cells, called neurons, in the outermost layer, called the cortex. Upon close examination (see Figure 10), we note that thin fibers, called dendrites, radiate from the body of the cell. Dendrites bring information (in the form of electrical impulses) *from* other neurons. Axons transfer information *to* other cells.

The juncture or connecting point between dendrites and axons is called the synapse or synaptic juncture.

Figure 10: Brain cells

A suitable analogy would be telephone wires connecting all of the telephones within a system and connecting multiple systems over the entire world.

This branching system of dendrites and its connecting points, or synapses, is largely, but not wholly, dependent upon the basic genetic architecture of our brains. Research tells us that it is the way in which this genetic structure of neurons interacts with the environment that provides the broad range of variations for learning and behavior.

As nerve cells receive input, they send out dendrite branches and new synapses are formed. Dendrites can also cease to exist, as we shall see! Interaction with the environment shapes the brain's potential for creating new connections.

The brain's information and processing capabilities are almost infinite in variation and complexity, with literally trillions of connections at the synapses of a normal brain. This provides an almost unlimited potential for learning, and is especially true in early childhood when the brain may contain as many as six times more connections (in a five-year-old) than exist in the brain of an adult.

Eventually, the brain is "pruned" or thinned of unused and unnecessary (overly redundant) dendrites and axons. This pruning is a normal and natural occurrence and indeed is a major neurological component of childhood in preparation for the adult years. This mass of potential has to be trimmed into networks of connections that lead to smooth, skillful, and automatic learning and behavior—in anything from learning to play a musical instrument or a new sport, to solving math problems or writing a book.

The type of processing network that a particular brain develops is directly related to the types of experiences to which an individual is exposed—especially in childhood.

In terms of the synapses themselves, it is the strength and efficiency of synaptic connections that determines the speed and power with which the brain functions. These synapses are formed, strengthened, and maintained by experience—the most important fact yet discovered about them. Different skills, behaviors, and responses are best learned at particular times in the development of the child. This relates to the malleability of response and the timing of input. It is well known that the brain loses its malleability for certain skills over time. As an example, adults often struggle to acquire foreign languages—especially accents and inflections. Such activity is much easier for the young.

Depending on how enriched (or impoverished) the environment of learning, we know that there will be not only different amounts of dendrite branching, but that the synaptic junctions will be affected. Enriched environments result in the dimensions of the synapse becoming larger and, therefore, more responsive and efficient.

Taken together, these dendritic and synaptic activities are vitally important and demonstrate the vast significance of varied environments and experiences in the childhood years.

Myelin and Maturation

Surrounding each of the neurons is a host of other cells responsible for providing nutrients and carrying away waste products from the neurons. In an enriched environment, we get more of these support cells because the nerve cells, themselves, are getting larger. These *glial* cells have another, more recently discovered function that bears importantly on learning. In any circumstance where new learning is occurring, a fatty-protein is secreted along the lining of the axon. This protein, called *myelin*, forms a sheath of insulating material serving the dual function of stabilizing learning and speeding up the processing of information. The myelin sheath acts as a superconductor of learning—fat being an excellent conducting medium in the brain.

This myelination process develops slowly during childhood and adolescence, in a gradual progression from lower-to-higher level systems for learning. While the order (lower-to-higher) is genetically programmed, the total of myelin seems to reflect levels of stimulation, or input, and response. In effect, there is an age-appropriate schedule for learning with respect to myelination. Prior to myelination, the particular region of the brain involved does not operate efficiently. Forced learning, in this regard, may result in mixed up patterns of learning. It is even possible for negative neural networks ("resistance circuitry") to develop, according to Healy.

While it isn't completely understood how myelination occurs, it is most likely that, as we learn a new skill, concept, or behavior—through practice and repetition—more and more myelination occurs. Eventually, of course, the concentrated practice is no longer necessary or important because we have "learned our lesson well." The unconscious mind (the autonomic nervous system, actually) has taken over the task.

A simple example would be learning, as a child, to ride a bicycle. It probably isn't too difficult to recall how much concentration and effort were once required to learn this complex skill.

> *The brain . . . periodically prunes away any unmyelinated axons during childhood. This evidently occurs because the brain has many systems of redundancy in early childhood. When this occurs, the unlimited possibilities for imagination and learning are reduced. The largest pruning evidently occurs around age eleven . . .*

It was precisely that concentrated effort that most likely activated the myelination process. Once the appropriate axons were sufficiently coated—through such practice—the stabilization of learning occurred, freeing us to ride the bicycle without paying much attention to the task. That learning is so stable, we are sometimes surprised at our ability to get on a bicycle and ride even when we haven't done so in years or even decades.

The brain, as stated earlier, periodically prunes away any unmyelinated axons during childhood. This evidently occurs because the brain has many systems of redundancy in early childhood. When this occurs, the unlimited possibilities for imagination and learning are reduced. The largest pruning evidently occurs around age eleven, in preparation for the more focused and more adult mental capacities that will be needed. With that in mind, it is fascinating to note here that the only known difference between Einstein's brain and that of an ordinary person is that his brain had more glial cells per given area. Since glial cells activate the myelination process, it seems reasonable to assume that Einstein entered adulthood with a greater capacity to make novel and creative "connections." He often described the important role that imagination played in his discoveries of the reality-shattering principles that govern the physical universe.

From all that we currently know and are learning about the brain's development, we can better understand the immense importance of providing our children with the greatest possible exposure to non-threatening and supportive environments, positive stimulating models, and varied opportunities to become actively involved in age-appropriate learning experiences. This, in effect, becomes a simple formula for fostering the limitless potential in each human being.

By focusing on and fostering young people's strengths and potential, we are simultaneously enhancing their resiliency.

So, reformatting the Cycle of Competence, we might express it as a formula:

Caring, supportive relationships and environments

+ opportunities to practice and apply new learning

= creative, intelligent, productive well-being

This is exactly what our society, with its enormous problems and challenges, needs from each of its members. To the extent that we do not foster this, we reap its opposite: destructiveness, ignorance and dependency. Because nature's plan seems to be to prune the brain in order to rid itself of system redundancies and unused or underused neural connections, it is in our best interest to provide safe, secure, stimulating and varied environments as early and as often as possible in childhood. Herein lies the preservation of creative potential and the foundation of intelligence on which our future civilization and culture depends.

The Neurochemistry of Learning and Well-being

The wonder of learning can be extended to another level of neurophysiology—brain chemistry. Much has been learned during the last decade about the operation of the brain as it relates to special chemicals called neurotransmitters, neuropeptides and neurohormones. The study of these various brain chemicals represents the leading edge of scientific inquiry in a number of diverse, but related fields—learning, behavior, addiction, nutrition, stress, and well-being.

We can begin by examining more closely the activity which occurs at the connecting points between neurons, known as the pre- and post-synaptic juncture.

Figure 11 illustrates a highly magnified view of a single axon, in this case, the presynaptic juncture. Note that between the axon and dendrite, at the site of one gap, or synapse, are dots which represent neurochemicals. These brain chemicals provide the basis for thought, memory, feeling, behavior—in short, all of the requirements for learning. To date, more than sixty of these specialized chemicals have been catalogued by brain scientists, who anticipate finding as many as 200 in the coming years. Among these sixty are several that play a key role in mood regulation and learning.

Three of them—acetylcholine, dopamine, and norepinephrine—serve to increase the activity of the brain. These are the so-called excitatory neurochemcials (those that "rev" us up), and they are balanced, more or less, by the inhibitory neurochemicals (those which settle us down) such as serotonin, endorphin, and gamma amino butiric acid (GABA). To the extent that there exists a plentiful supply and balance of these brain chemicals, we enjoy healthy interactions with the environment. That is, we think, respond, and feel in ways that are harmonious with and appropriate to the situation. Fortunately, most of us are genetically endowed with the capacity to produce sufficient levels and balanced interactions of these chemicals to cope with life's various demands and opportunities.

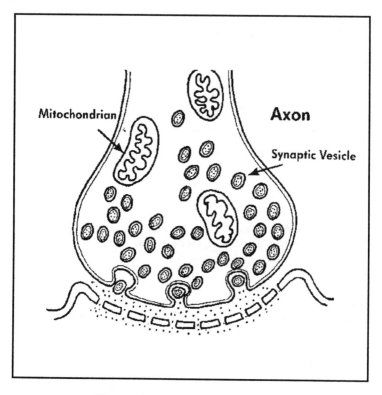

Figure 11: The Structure of an Axon

If we were to conceptualize, for simplicity's sake, a "vessel" containing these essential neuro-transmittors (Figure 11) we could then compare extreme scenarios for the human ability to respond adaptively and adequately—which, after all, is the basic feature of human intelligence.

In this figure, we can see at a glance the implications of a best and worst case scenario involving factors known to influence well-being, hardiness, and resilience. We know this to be the case because of recent discoveries in the new medical field of psychoneuroimmunology, to which we will turn our attention shortly.

Long-term Consistent Behavior

A central tenet of brain chemistry and how it affects overall well-being, can best be understood by contemplating a phrase emphasized by the noted psychopharmacologist and lecturer, Dr. Joel Robertson[10]:

Long-term, consistent behavior alters the base-line function of the brain.

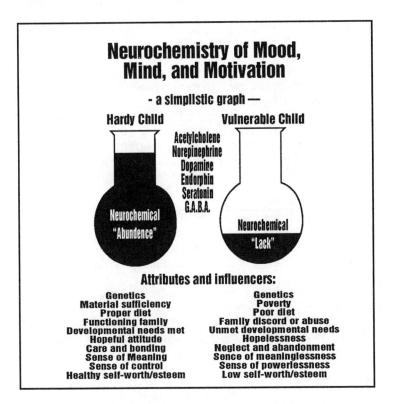

Figure 12: Genetic and Environmental Influences

This cogent phrase, it seems to me, summarizes a key finding in brain science relative to understanding such diverse phenomena as addiction and recovery (Dr. Robertson's area of expertise), high-level wellness, psychosomatic or stress-related illnesses, meditation, the "relaxation response," and learned optimism (or pessimism). In short, anything that defines our thinking, feeling and behavioral capacities.

To use an illustration from the field of addiction, consider the net effects of prolonged alcohol or other drug abuse on the brain. Today, we understand that the mood shift occurring when one takes a drink or a drug is caused by the actions of the alcohol or other drug on pre- or post-synaptic sites where brain chemicals are stored and released in order to "excite" or "inhibit" central nervous system activity. The pleasurable feeling that occurs is related to the location in the brain that a particular drug targets. In short, drugs, including alcohol, don't *cause* the mood change, they *trigger* it by manipulating these neurochemicals.

As dose and frequency levels of use exceed the central nervous system's capacity to replenish stored mood-altering neurotransmitters released by the alcohol or drugs, there is an overall deleterious effect on thinking and feeling. The affected individual initially enjoys the fact that various drugs are readily "triggering" positive mood changes. In the long run (or short run for fast-acting, high-potency drugs such as crack cocaine), this kind of "consistent behavior" alters the brain's baseline functioning. In this case, for the worse.

The opposite is true in recovery. Long-term consistent positive behavior—abstinence, exercise, healthy outlook, good nutrition, etc.—eventually brings the brain back to an improved level of functioning. Unless, of course, there has been damage.

Scientists have the capacity to actually quantify these changes by using blood or urine workups to analyze the metabolic by-products of essential neurotransmitters. This, in fact, is a practice currently in use by some practitioners to monitor actual client progress in recovery from chemical addictions.

Applying the implications of these exciting discoveries to a theory of childhood resilience, or to the field of prevention, we can say that any positive alteration in the environment of a young person, done in an on-going or consistent manner, ought to improve the overall well-being of the affected person. Furthermore, positive change can beget positive change in the same manner that negative changes tend to foster more negative changes. The key to one or the other is "long-term, consistent behaviors." This implies, of course, an environment that supplies support and ample opportunities for bonding, practice, and involvement—the very foundations of resilience.

Psychoneuroimmunology

This new field of scientific investigation into human health is actually a synthesis of three fields of inquiry: psychology, brain science, and immunology. In essence, it explores the interactive relationship between our attitudes or beliefs, the chemistry of the central nervous system, and the resulting state of health. This field is beginning to validate and centralize the role of the mind in human health, formerly thought to have no bearing whatever on the body, at least, according to the bias of traditional medical science.

Critics of the field, in fact, maintain the older position that views the body as a machine over which the mind has little or no effect. This view is increasingly more difficult to maintain in light of recent findings. The purpose in highlighting some of these intriguing discoveries is to establish a more credible basis upon which to build on-going and wide-spread support and enthusiasm for the promotion of childhood protective factors.

Psychoneuroimmunology, or PNI, research has focused on the role of certain brain chemicals called neuropeptides. These important hormonal messengers are secreted by the brain, by the immune system, and by the nerve cells found in a variety of other organs. Interestingly enough, the areas of the brain that are involved in emotional responses (the limbic cortex) are especially rich in receptor sites for these chemicals.

Present in brain, body, and immune system, is a completely interactive process by which emotional states are gauged, thoughts are responded to, and the immune system reacts—for better or for worse. We are fast becoming heir to a whole new scientific view which indicates that love, happiness, and hope have a subtle, but profound effect on the body's ability to defend itself and maintain health.

In her best-selling book, *Minding the Body, Mending the Mind*, Dr. Joan Borysenko[11] recounts the amazing discoveries in which she was involved while director of the Mind/Body Clinic, New England Deaconess Hospital, Harvard Medical School. Highlighting a number of these would, I think, serve us well in establishing an important connection between human resiliency and health-promoting environments.

Calling upon the ground-breaking research of Dr. Herbert Benson on the role of hypothalmic functioning in human stress, Dr. Borysenko recounts the early discoveries connecting stress

> *Stress in any form releases energy-providing hormones such as adrenalin and cortisol which strongly inhibit the function of the immune system. This response is known as immunosuppression. Ironically, this natural response to a perceived threat, while fulfilling nature's design to keep us alert to successfully fight or evade a predator, has a net effect of reducing our ability to maintain long-term health.*

and anxiety to illness. Stress in any form releases energy-providing hormones such as adrenalin and cortisol which strongly inhibit the function of the immune system. This response is known as immunosuppression. Ironically, this natural response to a perceived threat, while fulfilling nature's design to keep us alert to successfully fight or evade a predator, has a net effect of reducing our ability to maintain long-term health. Thus, too much stress leads directly to musculo-skeletal tension and reduced immune system response. These, in turn, lead to aches, pains, and a variety of bodily disorders.

While the body is designed to recover quickly and well from the physiological responses to acute stress, it is long-term, or *chronic* stress that can jeopardize emotional and physical well-being. Perhaps the most debilitating form of chronic stress is that which is caused by two mental states—conditioned negative attitudes and feelings of helplessness and hopelessness. Dr. Borysenko points out that constant feelings of helplessness can throw off the balance of the endocrine, or hormone system. It elevates the immuno-suppressant corticoid hormones while simultaneously depleting the brain of the important neurotransmitter, norepinephrine, one of the brain chemicals necessary for feelings of contented well-being and happiness. Of even greater importance, are the studies demonstrating that the inability to *feel in control of stress* is more debilitating than the stressful event itself. The feeling of helplessness in the face of stress is most debilitating and damaging to immune system health.

These findings are reinforced by the profoundly important book, *Learned Optimism*, by Dr. Martin Seligman[12]. In describing the role of psychological states upon health, Dr. Seligman maintains that depression and pessimism worsen health in both the short run and the long term. He describes a chain of events that seem to be inextricably linked to poor health, beginning with a particular set of bad events—loss, failure, defeat—those that typically make us feel helpless and hopeless. He then describes the changes that occur simultaneously in the central nervous system; again, depletion of certain brain chemicals known to play a key role in keeping the immune system healthy. This depletion is, by now, a familiar theme—recall the effects of mood-altering drugs on brain chemicals. Stress can and does have the very same effects, although it takes longer for the deleterious effects to become manifest.

The body is constantly exposed to pathogens (germs that can make us ill) from the environment, but they are normally held in check by the immune system. However, when the immune system is partly shut down, and, therefore, less responsive to these harmful invaders, the pathogens go wild and disease becomes far more likely.

Dr. Seligman concludes, after assuring us that every link in the chain of causality is scientifically testable, by stating *"Therapy and prevention can work at each link."* That is to say that nothing is a given. Change and health are largely within our control.

After all, it is a well-known tenet of stress research that 90 percent of all stress is perceptual, while only ten percent is environmental (such as noise or toxic pollution.) This means that ninety percent of stress is always within our control.

Good health, then, is physical resiliency—the body's ability to bounce back from challenge, stress, and adversity. Since so much of physical health and well-being is dependent on our perceptions of and emotional responses to life events, it is clear that certain childhood protective factors play a role far more vital to the health of our communities and society than we might at first recognize or assume. The good news is that most of these factors are within our control.

Ultimately, the vitality and health of children is determined by genetics, environment, behavior, and attitude. Not everyone has the same health-promoting and sustaining mix of genes—some are far more susceptible to disease and depression, for example, than others. Genetics are indisputably important and, while we may or may not be able to fully and effectively counter a weak genetic constitution, many scientists argue that more important to successful adaptation is proper environment, attitude, and behavior. These latter factors are much more within our realm of influence and control.

A central dynamic to choice and creative response is a sense of control. While not specifically using the term "resilience," Dr. Borysenko makes the link between life's challenges and the ability to bounce back when she states:

"Most of us eventually will feel that life is out of control in some way. Whether we see this as a temporary situation whose resolution will add to our store of knowledge and experience or as one more threat demonstrating life's dangers is the most crucial question both for the quality of our life and our physical health."

This quotation brings to mind Joseph Chilton Pearce's admonition that the central organizing factor behind growth in intelligence is unconditional love and acceptance. The key to human well-being seems to lie in the nature of one's perceptions of threat versus love and acceptance.

The matrix for this is a sense of belonging, meaning, and active involvement with the forces that are attempting to influence us. The exciting field of psychoneuro immunology has provided a timely way to understand the significance of how attitude and belief, brain and physiological function, and principles of health interact to create a state of vulnerability or resilience and well-being.

To conclude this section, it is clear that childhood today is an institution at grave risk. The nature of this risk is seen in the myriad symptoms, from rising rates of teen pregnancy to increased levels of violence among the young. The origins of this risk are to be found in two factors disruptive to childhood well-beging, one following from the other.

One is the changing nature of society and family which has resulted in a widening gap between adults and children. The other has to do with the unmet developmental needs of many children and is directly related to this widening gap. An attempt was made to ground concerns about these changes in research related to childhood development, central nervous system functioning, learning theory, and mind-body principles of health.

In short, we have explored the dangers inherent in the crisis threatening our children. It is now time to explore the *opportunity* side of the crisis. It is time to look at the phenomena of childhood resilience—children who beat the odds and overcame adversity of various kinds.

Section 2:
A Shift in the Wind:
Moving from Risk to Resilience

Chapter 5: An Emerging Paradigm

The dominant view or paradigm of human development, as we in the Western world have come to know it, is both limited and limiting. It is a paradigm which, until very recently, has focused almost exclusively, on the pathological and defective side of our nature. This orientation makes sense when one considers the origin of mainstream ideas, theories, and practices of psychology and medicine.

What is sometimes called First Force and Second Force psychology refers to Freudian psychoanalytic and Skinnerian behavioral psychologies. These two insightful, but limited, perspectives on human nature received widespread acceptance and application at the precise historical moment when many members of our society became most vulnerable and needy—the decade of the 1950's!

The pathology/deficiency model

Let's review the unique events of the 1950's.

During this time, there was a massive migration of the population from rural America, with its multiple systems of support, to the urban and suburban environment, where the traditional extended families, close-knit communities, and long-term friend-

ships were no longer the norm. As a direct result of this population shift and diminished support, stress increasingly became
a way of life as people struggled with these environmental
changes.

In the absence of support, the normal problems and challenges
of living—childraising, earning a living, etc.—became magnified. In direct response to this, two things occurred:

- chemical use and abuse began to increase

- mental health problems increased among the new suburban population

In the 1950's, tranquilizers became a popular method of coping
with stress, and the consumption of alcohol increased markedly.
Despite the denial that characterized our society during this and
future decades, the massive social changes of the urban migration took its toll.

When people sought help or treatment for their problems in the
1950's, the two predominant paradigms of psychology were
Freudian and Skinnerian. Both of these paradigms are rather
gloomy in their assumptions about human nature.

Freudian psychology was based on the insight that we are ruled
by unconscious drives that are largely sexual or fear-based. This
view held that we have little or no control over our behavior
and actions because our motivations for them are unknown to
us. They are, by definition, unconscious. Thus, we are power-
less to change and master our own destiny in the face of these
largely hidden drives and urges. Unless, of course, we undergo
psychoanalysis to become conscious of these hidden forces.

Skinnerian psychology is based on the theory that people are
controlled by a reward and punishment mechanism. That is to
say that events outside of us (more or less the opposite of Freud's
view) *condition* us to act and respond in a certain manner. This
is also a fairly stultifying viewpoint that minimizes a person's
sense of self-control, self-determination, or sense of efficacy in
the world.

Taken together, the Freudian and Skinnerian ideas become the
basis for what might be called the *pathology/deficiency paradigm*.

The pathology/deficiency model of human development and behavior is, therefore, concerned with and focused on: (a) identifying those elements in one's personality that are not operating according to a norm (the pathology) or (b) identifying those elements that are lacking altogether (the deficiency). The chart in Figure 13 compares the focus of the pathology/deficiency model to the resilience/competency model that we will be discussing later.

1950 - 1963 Enormous Social Change	Freud Skinner	Initial Research: E. Werner M. Rutter N. Garmezy
1963 - 1970's Denial and Delusion	Tertiary Prevention AODA Treatment Hospitalization Labeling Diagnosing Rehabilitation	Concept rejected; Work continues: W. Beardslee J. Segal Seligman
1980's Support and Recovery	Intervention Co-Dependence ACOA 12 Steps Family Dysfunction Inner Child Grief	Risk and Protective Factors Identified Primary Prevention
1990's Empowerment		Resiliency Hardiness Wellness

Figure 13: Pathology vs Resiliency Model

In the 1960's and 1970's, to assist in the process of identification, practitioners became very adept at diagnosing and labeling human pathology. The *Diagnostic and Statistical Manual*, a thick compendium of codes that identify everything that, seemingly, can go wrong in a human being was developed and refined. An increasing number of people were hospitalized and treated for a variety of mental, emotional, and addictive disorders. We attempted to rehabilitate the young who were suffering from all manner of problems. In other words, we did a great deal of *tertiary prevention,* to use a term borrowed from the public health model.

To clarify:

- Tertiary prevention is what is done to treat a problem once it has become firmly established.

- Secondary prevention is the steps taken to intervene at an early point in the progression of a disease or epidemic.

- Primary prevention is what is done to keep problems from occurring to begin with.

In essence, we waited for the problems to reach critical proportions before we intervened. This is a bit like the notion expressed in an old cartoon I once saw of cars speeding along an elevated highway. There is a sudden and abrupt end to the highway and cars can be seen flying off the end to crash in a heap on top of other cars that preceded them over the brink. There, next to the pile of crashed cars and mangled bodies, is a line of ambulances to take away the casualties.

Tertiary prevention is what we put into effect to heal, repair, cure, remediate, rehabilitate, or otherwise try to fix once there is a serious problem. In the cartoon example, it is sending in the ambulances. Primary prevention would be investing the time, resources, and energy into finishing or extending the highway.

This approach to our growing social problems was not surprising. As Americans, we have always characterized ourselves and been described by others as an optimistic people. While this is laudable and to be appreciated, we are also distinguished by a very marked tendency towards *denial.*

It is in the nature of denial to ignore one's problems or pretend that they do not exist, only to discover at times that the problem is so serious that only massive infusions of effort can effect a change. Such was the growing state of affairs in the 1950's. In the 1960's and 1970's, we attempted to rectify the situation through tertiary prevention.

In the 1980's, there was more of a shift toward *secondary* prevention. For example, we set up student assistance teams in schools to identify young people who were involved with drugs and alcohol, taking our cue from the increasing successes that businesses were having with employee assistance programs . We learned a great deal about support and recovery, co-dependency, and family dysfunction as millions of people found their way to 12-step and other recovery programs during this decade.

This may well go down in the history of the 20th century as one of its largest social movements. Unlike other outwardly focused movements, this one had as its focus inner healing, peace, and serenity. To me, this focus was, perhaps, the most intriguing and important outgrowth of the pathology/deficiency/damage model because so many people found a way towards greater support and connectedness—the precise remedy for what was a principle deficit of the 1950's.

Clearly, benefits were realized during the period of delayed interventions and actions associated with tertiary prevention, rehabilitation, hospitalization, and so forth. There were successes. Many individuals have been and will continue to be helped by sincere and highly skilled therapists, rehabilitation and treatment specialists, and case-workers of all types. But the support and recovery movement of the 1980's has been a sorely-needed and sincerely appreciated outgrowth of the damage-control model of human behavior.

Yet, having said this, it is important to note the shortcomings of this viewpoint and approach. Consider, for example, the "success" rate (usually defined as at least one year of continuous sobriety) for adolescent substance abuse treatment. Currently, only about twelve to eighteen percent of young persons treated actually succeed. This means that the majority continue to struggle, and their conditions often become worse.

Common sense tells us that delayed intervention or action makes success more difficult to achieve. Not as obvious are the limitations imposed by the underlying assumptions.

The chart in Figure 14 summarizes the deficiency paradigm with its underlying assumptions.

	Pathology/ Deficiency Model
Based on:	Medical or disease model
Focus:	Maladaptation pathology illness deficiency
Research Design:	Retrospective Predisposing risk factors
Predicts:	Both problems and damage

Figure 14: Deficiency Model Focus and Characteristics

The pathology/deficit model focuses on an individual's maladjustment, insufficiency, or illness. This is a natural outgrowth of the medical/psychiatric model developed from studies of the sick or dead (in the case of medicine), and neurotic or psychotic (in the case of psychiatry). Research that supported the development of this paradigm used the retrospective approach. In this approach, we look at individuals who are currently experiencing a problem, such as disease, addiction or criminality. We then go backwards in time to find a set of circumstances or events in those persons' past that can be identified as coincidentally or causally related to the problem.

Based on these findings, this model has developed a certain capacity for predicting outcomes. In this case, the problems that can develop when a certain known set of conditions occur. For example, we know that there is a greater tendency for children of alcoholics to develop alcohol problems or life adjustment problems than for children from families without alcohol-related difficulties. This greater likelihood is considered to be, in a sense, predictive for an *entire* group, if we are not careful.

Having thus identified factors and possibly established a theory about the cause of the problem, a treatment protocol is set up and carried out, hoping to effect a cure or significant positive change.

Interestingly, in the 1950's, when Freudian and Skinnerian methods of treatment were being developed and implemented, other people—many of whom were trained in the pathology model—looked outside of the paradigm for *something else*. They evidently saw the limitations of the model and felt constrained by its sometimes rigid adherence to a partial and incomplete view of human development and growth. That "something else" they looked for would eventually become the resiliency/competency model.

The Resiliency Model

The roots of the resiliency model are partly to be found in the 1950's when Emmy Werner[13] and her associates set up a research project on the island of Kauai. The subjects of the study were 698 children, born in 1955. These children were tracked periodically for the next 30 years to determine the long-term consequences for children who experienced prenatal and perinatal stress, as well as other stressors in the family and community environment. The objective was to assess the results of adverse child-rearing conditions on children's overall development.

In her writings, Werner acknowledges how rare it was to conduct such an inquiry in the 1950's. As she points out, most investigators at that time concerned themselves with events that had culminated in human problems by looking at the history of individuals who were suffering from the problems. Once again, this retrospective approach can create the impression that the outcome is inevitable, since it takes into account only the "casualties", not the survivors.

By monitoring the life course of all the children born in a given place and period, a different set of conclusions would ultimately be derived about the nature of vulnerability, risk factors, and protective factors in childhood.

Werner, for example, was one of the first to find that despite such challenges as poverty, discordant home life, uneducated, addicted, or mentally ill parents, there were sizable numbers (fully one third) of the 200 or so highest risk children who went on to develop healthy personalities, stable careers, and strong interpersonal relations. Eventually, she and her research team identified key protective factors at work in the child-rearing environment. These protective elements included those found within the family, outside the family, and within the resilient children themselves.

> *They found that most of the children who grew up with the odds against them successfully overcame adversity. These children had or developed the resources to bounce back. In the words of Norman Garmezy, these were children who "worked well, played well, loved well, and hoped well," despite the obstacles and hardships that they had to overcome. It is in these and other studies that the terms "resilient children," "stress-resistant children," "ego-hardy children," and "vulnerable but invincible children" begin to appear.*

Those within the family included, for example, four or fewer children with a space of two years or more between them; the close, loving attention of a caretaker during the first years of life; and structure and rules in the household.

The protective elements external to the family included, among others, being well liked by classmates; having at least one close friend (usually several close friends); an informal network of neighbors, peers, and elders for counsel and support during challenging and difficult times. In short, resilient children seemed most able to find many sources of emotional support outside their immediate families.

Listening to Weiner, we get a clear sense of how refreshingly different is her approach and discovery: "Our findings . . . suggest that a number of potent protective factors or buffers have a more generalized effect on the life course of vulnerable children than do specific risk factors on stressful life events . . . [and] they offer us a more optimistic outlook."

During this same time period, Michael Rutter[14] and Norman Garmezy[15] conducted similar research in England and parts of the United States, respectively. Rutter, for example, studied resilient children growing up in homes with a mentally ill parent. He found many of the same protective factors that Werner discovered and also came to the conclusion that the timing of life's events and their particular meaning to a child were important in determining if the result would be beneficial or not.

These researchers and others noted a wonderful phenomenon. They found that *most* of the children who grew up with the odds against them, successfully overcame adversity. These children had or developed the resources to bounce back. In the words of Norman Garmezy, these were children who "worked well, played well, loved well, and hoped well," despite the obstacles and hardships that they had to overcome. It is in these and other studies that the terms "resilient children," "stress-resistant children," "ego-hardy children," and "vulnerable but invincible children" begin to appear.

According to the pathology/deficiency model, many, if not most of these children should have suffered from major problems because of their negative early childhood experiences. What the researchers found, instead, was that there were marked, and frequent, exceptions to the rule.

For example, Werner reported that findings appeared to demonstrate risk factors and stressful environments do not inevitably lead to poor adaptation. In fact, so long as the balance between stressful life events and protective factors is in the child's favor, successful adaptation is a distinct possibility. Many of the highest-risk children in her survey developed into "competent, caring, and confident people" who were capable of taking advantage of opportunities to improve themselves and benefit others.

Through the 1960's and 1970's, people such as William Beardslee[16], Julius Segal[17], and Martin Seligman[18] continued to do research in the emerging area of resiliency, while others joined their ranks and began to share and consolidate their findings.

Then in the 1980's, researchers such as David Hawkins[19], Richard Catalano, and their associates began to clearly and concisely link risk and protective factors together, making the work of practitioners easier. In effect, practitioners were provided with a set of precepts to follow that were known to be protective of at-risk youth.

Primary prevention grew in earnest in the 1980's. Its philosophical foundation is increasingly grounded in the competency/resiliency model. I believe that we are now on the verge of shifting the emphasis of our approach to young persons from the older pathology model to the newer one of resilience. It is a shift, most evident in the work being done by primary preventionists in the nation's schools and it holds forth a great deal of promise.

The chart below compares the historical development of the pathology and resiliency models.

	Pathology/ Deficiency Model	Resilience/ Competency Model
Based on:	Medical or disease model	Wellness model
Focus:	Maladaptation pathology deficiency illness	adaptation positive health sufficiency wellness
Research Design:	Retrospective Predisposing risk factors	Prospective Predisposing protective factors
Predicts:	Problems	Solutions

Figure 15: Competency Model and Characteristics

To sum up the underlying tenets of the competency/resiliency model, we can say that it is based on the study of *adaptivity*. It focuses on how human beings adapt, and consequently, on how they stay healthy. It is concerned with strengths, with what helps people bounce back, and what makes us stronger. It is, essentially, a wellness model.

Furthermore, the resiliency model studies people within an ecology. Unlike the pathology model that focuses more on the individual as an isolated unit, the resiliency model looks at the transactions between an individual and the family, the community, culture, and the environment. It is more of a holistic, ecological model, which says that one cannot look at children in isolation from environmental factors and influences.

The research design frequently employed is also quite different from that used to develop theories under the pathology model. Much of the research in the competency/resiliency model has been "prospective" or longitudinal. It builds theory by observing human development across time.

Thus, while the older model of damage, deficiency, and pathology provided a useful and partially successful approach to solving human health problems, it affords us an incomplete and, therefore, limiting view of ourselves and our potential for development.

Rediscovering Assets: A Study for Our Time

The need to shift our emphasis from the pathology model to the resiliency model can be seen in the study entitled "The Troubled Journey—a Profile Of American Youth."[20] Conducted by a research team from The Search Institute in Minneapolis, Minnesota, the study was headed by Dr. Peter Benson.

The original study included 47,000 students in the sixth through twelfth grades, who lived in 111 primarily small communities across twenty-five states. (In this case, communities with populations of less than 100,000.)

The findings were quite similar to those in other reports that tend to look at national data, using a larger, urban base for the study. Currently, the study includes more than 250,000 young persons.

Included at the outset of the report were four criteria that, when taken together, were found to be indicative of "well-being" in youth. These criteria were:

- Having twenty or more of thirty assets

- Having two or fewer of ten deficits

- Having two or fewer of twenty at-risk indicators

- Doing at least one hour per week of pro-social behavior

The study found that only about ten percent of the young people surveyed met the minimal criteria for overall well-being. While this does not mean that ninety percent of our youth will definitely develop problems, it does mean that a huge number of children are vulnerable to some degree. This is consistent with other findings that tell us the vast majority of young people are at risk.

Again quoting the authors, "We cannot be sure what long-term consequences are in store for the ninety percent who fail to meet the criteria. Fortunately, some will thrive. And some, unfortunately, will carry over into adulthood some scar or behavioral tendency that will stifle productivity."

In short, they are at-risk of not living up to their full emotional, intellectual, economic, vocational, or spiritual potential.

It is instructive to examine more closely each of these areas in turn highlighting some of the salient discoveries of this rather large and compelling report.

Assets

An *asset,* according to the study, is a factor that promotes positive development in youth. External assets include positive relationships with school, friends, family and community. Internal assets include personal convictions, values, and attitudes.

The authors of the study tell us that *external* assets are temporary supports that we give to children until they have developed a strong set of *internal* assets. The external assets provide a firm foundation for children to build on. A useful analogy is the scaffolding used to put up the walls of a brick building. Once in place, the walls of the building no longer require the scaffold, though it was essential in the construction phase.

The chart below lists the sixteen external assets. Complete definitions of each asset can be found in Appendix A.

	External Assets		External Assets
1	Parental support	9	Parental discipline
2	Parents as social resources	10	Parental monitoring
3	Parental communication	11	Time at home
4	Other adult resources	12	Positive peer influence
5	Other adult communication	13	Involvement in music
6	Parental involvement in schooling	14	Involvement in school extra-curricular activities
7	Positive school climate	15	Involvement in community organizations or activities
8	Parental standards	16	Involvement in religious activities

Figure 16: External Assets
Used by permission of The Search Institute

External assets are divided into three broad categories:

- Care and support (1-7)

- Monitoring and control (8 -12)

- Structured use of time (13 - 16)

The next chart lists the fourteen *internal* assets. Complete definitions of each asset can also be found in Appendix A.

	Internal Assets		Internal Assets
1	Homework	8	Places value on sexual restraint
2	Educational aspiration	9	Assertiveness skills
3	School performance	10	Decision-making skills
4	Achievement motivation	11	Planning skills
5	Concern about world hunger	12	Friendship-making skills
6	Satisfaction derived from helping people	13	Self-esteem
7	Care about other people's feelings	14	Positive view of personal future

Figure 17: Internal Assets
Used by permission of The Search Institute

Internal assets are also divided into three major categories.

- Educational aspirations (1-4)

- Positive values (5 - 8)

- Social competencies (9-14)

Dr. Benson reports that, overall, in some specific areas, young persons are in pretty good shape. For example, seventy-five percent indicated that parental standards were sufficient, while seventy-seven percent agreed that parental monitoring was also adequate.

On the other hand, only thirty percent of students perceived school as having a "positive climate," and a similar low percentage was reported for positive peer influence. Only twenty-six percent reported parental involvement in schooling.

In a similar vein, some inner assets were found to be common among youth—achievement motivation, educational aspirations, caring about other people's feelings, assertiveness skills—while other assets were disappointingly low. These included homework and valuing sexual restraint.

The study found that the average student possess only sixty percent of the defined external assets and only fifty percent of the vitally important internal assets. Obviously, this is far from desirable and a very troubling finding.

Deficits

The term *deficit*, in this study, refers to those factors that inhibit healthy development, thereby making young people more vulnerable. Specifically, Dr. Benson's team found 10 key deficits associated with high-risk behaviors. These deficits are listed in the chart below.

	Deficits		Deficits
1	Stress at home or in school	6	Physical abuse
2	Hedonistic values focusing on self-serving values	7	Sexual abuse
3	Over-exposure to TV (more than 3 hours per day)	8	Parental addiction
4	Drinking party attendance on a regular basis	9	Social isolation
5	Excessive time at home alone (more than 2 hours per day)	10	Negative peer pressure

Figure 18: Deficits
Used by permission of The Search Institute

Only eight percent of the students studied had zero deficits. Almost fifty percent had three or more, which places these children above the threshold for an at-risk situation. The study team also found that some of the deficits tend to increase over time. Drinking parties, sexual abuse, and high stress during the early teens tend to increase as the child gets older.

The collective picture was disconcerting. The majority of teens surveyed had too few assets and too many deficits, with some assets actually diminishing in the later school years. Evidently, just at the time when teens most need the external support systems, those systems begin to disappear or are underutilized, leaving the teens more vulnerable.

A third area of study focused on the actual risk behaviors of teens—termed *risk-indicators* in the report. These were described briefly in the first section of this book on multiple risk factors affecting young persons. (For a fuller definition of each, please see Appendix B.)

The study showed that these behaviors increase rather dramatically as students get older; with drinking and sexually related behaviors, not surprisingly, being the most dramatic. As indicated in an earlier chapter of this book the report also established that students at risk in one area have a greater likelihood of being at risk in other specific areas.

Finally, the authors hasten to point out the fact that the sample did not include the urban poor or students who have dropped out of school. Adding these two groups would certainly have increased the percentage substantially, according to the report.

A Study in Hope

Although these statistics seem dismal on the surface, the study contains a welcome and ultimately hopeful conclusion. Dr. Benson and his researchers discovered that each increase in assets in a young person's life cuts at-riskness in half. The chart below illustrates the number of high risk behaviors exhibited by children grouped according to the number of assets they possessed.

Those students who had fewer than eleven assets were involved in four or more risk behaviors, such as, drinking, taking drugs, depression, and involvement in anti-social actions. In contrast, those who had the highest number of assets were involved in remarkably few risk behaviors.

Assets	Risk Indicators
1-10	4
11-20	2
21-25	1
26-30	0.5

*Figure 19: Assets vs Risk Indicators
Used by permission of The Search Institute*

The conclusion derived from this is that *assets suppress at-riskness.* This is an exciting and significant finding. The three decades we spent trying to drive down risk behaviors or trying to treat the results of risk behaviors, were not very successful.

Our best efforts to rehabilitate, remediate, and treat problems once they appeared have left us frustrated and dismayed. The conclusions drawn from this study strongly support the idea that we need to think and act in a different manner.

Focus on building assets

The need now is to focus on how to build assets and strengths in children while eliminating deficits. In the building of those strengths, we expect to find a natural diminishing effect on potential risk behaviors.

Psychologists have known for more than thirty years, that the way to grow capable, competent, and successful people is to help them to develop their strengths and *not* by focusing on their weaknesses. Having by now fully experienced the limitations of the earlier paradigm, I believe we may be ready to embrace the admonitions of those early psychologists.

The Search Institute study can help us to transition from the pathology model, which focused on damage and deficiency, to a model which focuses on building strengths, and wellness.

Based on their findings, a set of recommendations were drawn up for parents, educators, and community leaders. Some of them are common sense and many are a reinforcement of what people are already doing. (Please see Appendix C.) All are essential components of well-being in young people.

Promoting Youth Development

"If we continue to believe that the only way to help 'at-risk' young people is to devote more resources to 'fixing' their problems, we will not only fail, but also seriously weaken an already fragile system of youth development supports. There is growing agreement that the high risk behaviors that have received so much public and political attention cannot be reduced without meeting youths' needs and cultivating their skills—in essence, without addressing the broader issue of youth development."[21]

The above statement was made by Karen J. Pittman, Director of the Center for Youth Development and Policy Research in Washington, D.C. before the House Select Committee on Children, Youth, and Family.

It echos, reinforces, and, in a sense, builds on the findings of Dr. Peter Benson's research team.

Pittman argues convincingly that the only way we can successfully contribute to youth development is to attend not only to the content of what they are learning, but to the environments in which the learning takes place. We can expect children to grow only by offering them opportunities to develop skills, contribute, achieve a sense of belonging, form close relationships, and explore new ideas while avoiding real risks.

Pittman goes on to say that the process of youth development goes far beyond academic competence through the formalized classroom learning process. It involves experiential and "real world" learning as well, and occurs through interaction with a variety of people (some positive and some negative) and places (again, some positive and some negative.) The interactions with people and places become, in effect, the agents for impacting a young person's overall sense of self-worth, membership, safety, and mastery.

By making youth development as real as youth problems, Pittman says, we can gain the attention and the respect of our youth. She reminds us, that what works for all youth in every community is a sustained and demonstrated commitment to helping young people see and achieve meaningful, positive goals.

Pittman's testimony concludes by citing the examples of four specific programs that fulfill the essential requisites for youth development. These programs and philosophies are consistent with the goal of developing healthy, vital, and empowered young people.

By creating a renewed vision of that which sustains the consistent, positive development of all youth, we revitalize our efforts. We move and act with the knowledge that we are on the right path. We feel empowered, knowing that we are empowering young people. By deepening our understanding of the concept, process, and elements of resilience, we can add the vital ingredients of renewed hope and increased faith to our spirit.

It is to a deeper understanding of childhood resilience that we turn next.

Chapter 6: Understanding Resilience

To begin this chapter on a somewhat personal note, the first time I encountered the idea of resilience as applied to children was in an article by William Beardslee[22]. Without knowing it then, I was about to experience a subtle, but significant, personal and professional paradigm-shift of my own. My view of myself and my work with young people would be increasingly altered as a result.

William Beardslee and the Three Factors in Resilience

William Beardslee discovered three factors related to resilience in the population that he studied. Specifically, his subjects were adolescents growing up in homes where there was alcoholism or mental illness in one or both parents. Beardslee studied teenagers who were successful in work, school, and relationships in spite of the serious adversity in the home environment. He discovered that all of the resilient teenagers had three things in common:

- A sense of humor and ability to have fun

- A sense of detachment (healthy distancing from the disorganizing or dysfunctional element or person in the family)

- The presence of one healthy adult

91

The power of one healthy adult

Beardslee noted that there must be one healthy adult (not necessarily a parent) who is in a position to provide *nurturing* and who can be a *mirror to reality*. As you recall from an earlier chapter, Urie Bronfenbrenner maintains that young people today have the highest level of alienation and anomie of any generation. Beardslee's discovery becomes, in essence, a counteracting force against these debilitating effects of our time.

The nurturing provided by the one healthy adult reduces alienation because nurturing is the basis of bonding. Nurturance and bonding reduce feelings of alienation. By acting as a mirror to reality, the healthy adult assists the young person in clarifying difficult feelings and challenges, while helping him or her to solve problems. In the process, the child learns positive skills for dealing with problems and challenges. This reduces the tendency toward anomie, which is a feeling of normlessness that expresses itself through a poorly developed internalized structure for coping with stress and dealing effectively with problems.

The healthy adult, identified by Beardslee as a requirement for resilience, is the personification of the essential ingredient that Bronfenbrenner says is missing in today's society. The truly miraculous part of the "recipe" is that, in many cases, it *only takes one adult!* The key, of course, is an adult who is consistently available and emotionally invested in the child.

I am continually astonished at the power of one adult in the life of a child. Could it be that so many children are engaging in high-risk behaviors because there is not one adult consistently there and emotionally involved with them in a healthy manner? The evidence from our fast-paced and depersonalized society certainly indicates just that.

Supporting the "healthy adult" concept is a recent book by Alice Miller[23], called *The Untouched Key*. This book uses psychohistories of the famous and the infamous to investigate why some children who were abused or traumatized bounced back to become creative and artistic while others became destructive. Her subjects include such diverse figures as Adolf

Hitler, Joseph Stalin, Fredrich Nietze, Pablo Picasso, and Buster Keaton.

In applying the tools of psychohistory to the childhoods of these well-known people, she found that those who overcame their abusive backgrounds and achieved well in artistic and creative areas shared one common element that was absent in those who turned to destruction. That common experience was the presence of what she called a *sympathetic witness*.

Miller describes the sympathetic witness as an adult who listens to and believes the child and the child's story. Miller discovered that, in the cases of such monstrously destructive per-

> *By acting as a mirror to reality, the healthy adult assists the young person in clarifying difficult feelings and challenges, while helping him or her to solve problems. In the process, the child learns positive skills for dealing with problems and challenges.*

sonalities as Hitler and Stalin, there was, evidently, not a single adult available to bear witness to the atrocious abuse they received at the hands of their fathers.

In many ways, we are all witnesses—or we can be. When we deal with our children, our students, our patients, and clients, we have the opportunity to bear witness to their pain and suffering. This can occur naturally in our interactions with them as long as we remain sensitive to their needs and their own timing, listening to and acknowledging the story that unfolds-both the small, everyday hurts, and the traumatizing ones as well. It could be the one thing in their lives that will help them heal and to bounce back.

The most common thread unifying the rich tapestry of childhood resilience and risk reduction is the enduring presence of a healthy adult. It shows up in the literature so often and is so consistent with what we know about childhood development and the nature of learning itself, that it may very well be the basis of resilience.

It might be considered the necessary, though not necessarily *sufficient*, condition of resilience. With the presence of an involved, healthy adult, every child can grow up healthy (though other factors, no doubt, contribute.)

The only alternative to the presence of this accessible, consistently invested adult—when such a person is unavailable either in the short or the long term—is a sibling, a friend, or a peer group that can fulfill the same human needs.

With this in mind, let us look at bit more closely at the dynamics of resiliency in human affairs.

A New Model of Human Development

Resiliency is the ability to bounce back, recover from, or adjust to misfortune or change.

This definition, coming straight from a standard desk dictionary, is profoundly important and almost a truism when applied to human beings. After all, it is the adaptive nature of Homo Sapiens that has enabled us, as a species, to survive and thrive so impressively. We are by our very nature, adjustable, bouncing back and flexibly adapting to the most extreme circumstances of change and misfortune that our planet and our fellow humans can conjure.

It may have been this obvious feature of our very nature that led Urie Bronfenbrenner to propose a timely and appropriate view of human development. In his transactional-ecological model of development, he says:

"The human personality is viewed as a self-righting mechanism that is engaged in active, ongoing adaptation to its environment."[24]

This implies that, given the right circumstances, all humans can bounce back adaptively *because it is part of our very nature to do so*. The nature of the human spirit, as Emmy Werner might well put it, is that we are "vulnerable, but invincible." In light of this, what is in fact remarkable is how *difficult* it can be to extinguish this natural and healthy tendency in most people. While some children and young people are clearly more vulnerable than others, most will, in fact, bounce back from adversity given the proper resources, support, and encouragement with which to do so.

One way to look at the dynamics of resilience is illustrated in the graphic below.

The graphic illustrates how the interaction between the individual and the environment can create resilience on the one hand, or dysfunction on the other. In this model, the challenges and stresses of life are held in balance by what the authors call biopsychospiritual *protective factors*. These protective factors include good genetics, healthy outlook, and other elements that characterize a healthy child.

The authors point out that if the stresses and protective factors are relatively equal, there is balance and we proceed in a balanced manner (homeostatically). The balance can be disrupted when some event or situation increases the stresses to the point where we are overwhelmed and become disorganized. This model encourages us to look at how being overwhelmed or falling apart *can be* the first step on the road to resiliency. The arrow can either move to the right as reintegration proceeds, or it can continue to move downward, toward depression, incarceration, illness, or even death.

The key factor in determining the direction in which an individual moves is *support*. Assuming that support exists, the likelihood is greater for successful reintegration. In a school setting, the support may take the form of a caring faculty member,

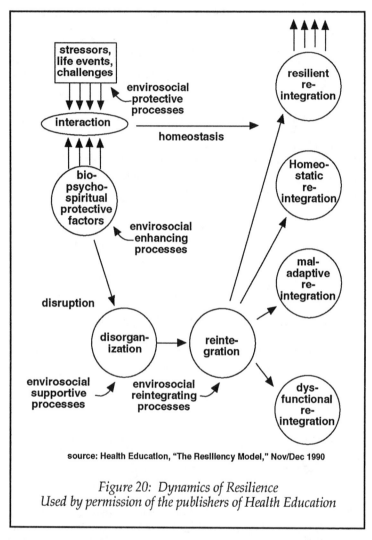

Figure 20: Dynamics of Resilience
Used by permission of the publishers of Health Education

counseling services, and/or support groups. At home it is a caring adult, a supportive neighbor, perhaps an extended family member who helps the young person pick up the pieces an go on. Undoubtedly, it begins with the presence of that "one healthy adult."

Looking at the right side of the diagram, we find that reintegration proceeds towards varying degrees of success:

- dysfunctional reintegration

- mal-adjustive reintegration

- homeostatic reintegration

- resilient reintegration

Dysfunctional reintegration is, I think, what we have been calling the pathology model. This diagram helps to put the pathology model in its appropriate context. It is potentially, though not necessarily, part of becoming resilient. For example, young people who are in drug treatment programs are learning new coping skills and attitudes that can help them to attain a greater degree of functionality as they go through the recovery process.

Resilient reintegration occurs when a child or adult has had to face adversity and, as a result, has acquired new skills, attitudes, or beliefs that allow for a higher level of functioning. We all face adversity, yet, for the most part, we do bounce back. What we need to do is create an atmosphere where there is as much support as possible for young people so that they do not become irretrievably damaged when the inevitable stresses overwhelm the current level of protective factors.

We do this constantly in small ways as well as large. Any time a child fails to make it onto a sports team or doesn't get a part in a play, there is disappointment and a sense of failure. When we provide support to help that child overcome the disappointment *and try again,* we have helped him or her to be resilient.

More than anything else, this model demonstrates the importance of *support* in fostering resilience. Even with support, some children become damaged, failing to bounce back from adversity. Without support, however, the likelihood is far greater that the "self-righting mechanism" will fail.

To better understand and appreciate the origins of this self-righting mechanism we turn to an analysis of key components involved in the resilience process.

Chapter 7:
The Resilient Child

Bonnie Benard and the Resilient Child Profile

Bonnie Benard is a well-known and highly-regarded research writer in the primary prevention field. She does a wonderful job of culling, synthesizing, and interpreting a great deal of timely and important research on topics related to reducing risk and enhancing protective factors for children, teens, and their families. In her widely circulated article "Fostering Resilience in Kids"[26], she provides a cogent overview of the most important factors related to resilience.

Benard describes four broad traits that characterize the resilient child:

- *Social competence*, in the form of responsiveness, empathy, flexibility, caring, communication skills, and a sense of humor. It is interesting to note that these are the very traits that appear to be conspicuously absent in addicts and criminals.

- *Problem solving skills* such as abstract thinking, developing alternative solutions, planning, and goal-setting. This applies to both the academic and social arena.

- *Autonomy* in the form of independence, a strong sense of self and identity, and a sense of mastery.

- *Sense of purpose and future.* A most important factor that includes a strong sense of educational achievement, strong goals, persistence, and a positive view of the future.

These four factors are listed in more detail in Figure 21.

Profile of the Resilient Child

Social Competence
        Responsiveness
        Flexibility
        Empathy/Caring
        Communication Skills
        Sense of Humor
Problem-solving Skills
        Critical thinking
        Generates alternatives
        Planning
        Produces change
Autonomy
        Self-esteem, self efficacy
        Internal locus of control
        Independence
        Adaptive distancing
Sense of Purpose and Future
        Goal directedness
        Achievement
        Motivation
        Educational Aspirations
        Healthy expectations
        Persistence
        Hopefulness
        Compelling future
        Coherence/meaningfulness

Figure 21: Profile of the Resilient Child

Source: "Fostering Resiliency in Kids: Protective Factors in the Family, School and Community," Bonnie Benard, Western Regional Center for Drug Free Schools and Communities

In short, because of these factors, the resilient child is one who, despite adversity, continues to "work well, play well, love well, and expect well."

A look at protective factors

The major determinant of whether a child becomes resilient or not, according to Benard, is the degree to which he or she experiences certain protective factors.

Protective factors are those traits, conditions, and situations, that alter or reverse potentially destructive outcomes. They are, in essence, positive action strategies. If we maximize protective factors, we maximize resiliency.

We find protective factors at home, in schools, and in the community. According to Benard, they fall into three broad categories:

- Caring and support

- High expectations

- Encouraging children's participation

Benard points out the importance of keeping in mind that resiliency research, by its very nature, looks at children and youth who are experiencing major stress, challenge, and adversity in one or more of the child-rearing institutions. Thus, the protective factors are to be found in or will derive from the healthier one or two of these three institutions. For example, if a child is at risk in the family due to abuse, neglect or alcoholism, it is the school or community that will be the source of protections and enhancement.

What follows is a summation of Benard's findings about environmental protective factors found in families and schools. Studies or findings mentioned are those that Benard, herself, described by way of meticulously making her case for fostering resilience in childhood. They offer meaningful and important strategies for promoting resiliency.

I refer the reader interested in a fuller explanation of family, community, and school strategies to Benard's original article.

(See also Appendix C for a summary of community protective factors recommended for fostering resilience.)

Family Protective Factors

When viewed in the context of the family, protective factors become a powerful predictor of the outcome for children and youth, according to Benard. And this comes as no surprise. The family characteristics listed below are primary determinants of positive outcomes.

Protective Factors Within the Family
"The Healthy Family"

Caring and Support

A close relationship with one person

Affection expressed physically and verbally

High Expectations

From early childhood

Structure and discipline

Order and clear expectations

Faith: Hope and expectations for the future

Values and encourages education

Opportunities for Participation

Valued participant in family activities

Domestic responsibilities

Encourages independence

Respect for child's autonomy

Figure 22: The Healthy Family

Caring and Support

Essentially, what this factor comes down to is a close relationship with at least one caring and healthy adult; one capable of expressing affection and who is consistently available to the child. Most important in this regard is the provision of stable care and adequate and appropriate attention in the first year of life.

Researchers maintain that the social relationships in the immediate care giving environment are, by far, the best predictors of children's behavioral outcomes. For example, Michael Rutter found that only 25 percent of children who grew up in troubled homes showed signs of conduct disorders *if* they had a single good relationship with a parent, as compared to 75 percent who lacked such a relationship. (A close relationship, in this case, was defined in terms of the presence of "high warmth and absence of severe criticism.")

In a similar vein, studies indicate that a most important variable in the impact on children of parental alcoholism is the supportiveness of the non-alcoholic parent. Furthermore, this kind of close relationship can even mitigate adolescent alcohol and other drug use.

As I stated earlier in various ways, it is the enduring presence of one healthy adult that plays predominately in the research on childhood resilience—indeed, it is the *necessary* condition for it.

High Expectations

So often the kinds of expectations we have for our children become prophetic. When we expect little of them, they do very little. Or worse, when we verbally and non-verbally dictate, suggest, or imply negative expectations—i.e. calling children stupid, worthless, incompetent, etc.—we unwittingly influence their personalities and behaviors in a possibly indelible fashion.

Conversely, Benard maintains, holding high expectations for children helps to explain why some children growing up in poverty, for example, still manage to be successful in school, work , and life as they mature into young adults.

Roger Mills' work with parents living in an impoverished housing project in Miami showed how parents, by communicating a positive attitude towards their ability to learn, played a key role in reducing problem behaviors (including substance abuse) among their children. These parents told their children "You have everything you need to be successful, and you can do it!" The key to high expectations, it seems, is to establish them when a child is very young.

Other aspects of high expectations in developing resiliency are the development of morality, along with a strong faith in a higher power. These factors help to provide a sense of perspective, understanding, patience, and perseverance that would otherwise be missing.

In addition, a sense of family structure, discipline, and clearly defined, humane rules and regulations help to establish a consistency and structure upon which children can develop their expectations for and about themselves. For example, studies of families characterized as *"authoritative"*—warm, supportive, with clear rules and expectations—had low rates of adolescent alcohol and other drug use, as compared to families that could be labeled "authoritarian" or "permissive."

Finally, we find in families that value and encourage education a predictor of positive outcomes in children. Children who have learned the value of education—formal or otherwise—tend to do better in various areas of their lives as they become adults. Education, however it is derived, provides the necessary knowledge, flexibility, and preparedness to succeed in work as well as in relationships and life in general.

Occasionally, the notion of high expectations serves to confuse rather than clarify an important dimension of resilience. Is it possible, as an example, for parents to hold expectations for their children that are too high and thus, potentially damaging? The answer is both Yes and No, I think.

In one sense, we know that too much structure, too many rules, and too many expectations can undermine a child and play a role in passivity and/or aggressive acting-out behaviors. Similarly, when we hold high expectations for our children's success—in any area of life—and then rigidly hold them accountable for their failure to measure up each step of the way, we are doing them a grave disservice.

What we really mean by high expectations is an attitude that we should be instilling in our young. It is the attitude or thought process that says: "I can do it! I have what it takes to succeed."

Perhaps the idea of high expectations could be rephrased as *positive* expectations, or *healthy and realistic* expectations. However, we need to be careful not to lose the spirit of the potential beneficial effects for our children when we do hold the highest vision for them. Certainly, its opposite—low expectations—can have a deleterious effect on some children.

Encouraging Participation

A key characteristic of the family backgrounds of resilient children reported in Benard's research is participation. In these families, children contributed in meaningful ways and had many opportunities to participate. Such things as assigned chores, domestic responsibilities, care of siblings, and part-time work to help support the family were sources of strength and character building for these children. When a child is provided with these kinds of responsibilities there can be no doubt about their worthiness and capability as family members. Children who are required to handle such tasks typically have a strong sense of belonging, importance, and significance.

Benard's central insight is two-fold. First, that the three protective factors that foster resilience in children—caring environments, high and clear expectations, and children being given lots of opportunities to participate meaningfully in the life of the family—are directly related to the four traits of resiliency: social competence, problem-solving skills, autonomy, and a sense of purpose. Secondly, she discovered in the literature, the existence of those same primary protective factors in the other two child-raising institutions: School and Community.

School Protective Factors

Caring and Support

A supportive school environment and a caring teacher can make an enormous difference in the life of a vulnerable child. As

Benard points out, "the level of care and support in a school is a powerful predictor of positive outcome for youth."[27] While only a few such studies evidently exist, those that do, according to Benard, provide a helpful buffer for children who overcome adversity.

It is a source of both delight and amazement to me—and very validating as well—to have participants in our workshops on resilience reflect upon and share with one another about a special teacher who truly made a difference in their lives. A recent study of school drop-outs bears significantly on this factor as well.

Evidently, a key finding was that very few, if any, of the drop-outs in the study could recall any teacher whom they could consider a friend throughout their school years.

> *From poor and disadvantaged children to children of wealthy parents who are raised principally in boarding schools, the literature seems to suggest the importance of caring peers and friends in the school environment.*

Benard cites a study conducted by James Coleman on effective schools. Coleman suggests that if schools were to accept more fully their role as an agent of families, with emphasis given to providing more care for the child through attention, personal interest, involvement, continuity and intimacy—children would develop more successfully in school and as adults.

In another related finding, Benard notes that peers can and often do provide a protective shield for one another. From poor and disadvantaged children to children of wealthy parents who are raised principally in boarding schools, the literature seems to suggest the importance of caring peers and friends in the school environment. Bernard cites two particularly large studies (meta-studies comparing the effects of more that 200 other studies) that underscore and support the significant role of peer programs in reducing substance abuse in youth.

Her conclusion: "Prevention programs which have focused on increasing the amount of social support available to youth in their schools by facilitating the development of teacher and peer relationships...unequivocally demonstrate [that] a care giving environment in the school serves as a 'protective shield'."[28]

High Expectations

Schools provide a protective shield, according to Benard, when they establish high expectations for all students, then act to support those students in achieving their goals. This school-wide *ethos* of high expectations (that includes emphasis on academic achievement, clearly stated rules, high student participation, and a variety of academic and extra curricular activities) figures prominently in successful schools. Benard quotes Michael Rutter who asserts: "schools that foster high self-esteem and that promote social and scholastic success reduce the likelihood of emotional and behavioral disturbance."

It was also found that successful schools minimized or eliminated altogether labeling and tracking of students. Some researchers have demonstrated that slow learners, for example, placed in accelerated learning programs were able to do well and even excel. So often students live up to (or down to) their label in a way that can only be described as a self-fulfilling prophesy. Clearly, it is the expectations of adults—in this case staff—and of the students themselves that determines so much of their future success.

As Benard puts it, "when the message one consistently hears—from family members, from teachers, from significant other in one's environment—is, 'You are a bright and capable person,' one naturally sees oneself as a bright and capable person, a person with that resilient trait: a sense of purpose and a bright future."[29]

Youth participation and Involvement

Holding high expectations for youth and providing them with opportunities to participate and become meaningfully involved go hand-in-hand. In the school setting, this means giving students ample opportunity to respond actively to teachers and with instructional resources.

Rutter found that schools with low levels of deviant acting-out behaviors were those that gave students plenty of responsibility, while providing all students with multiple opportunities to discover something they could succeed in. Other researchers found that this combination served as a protective factor against alcohol and other drug abuse as well.

By actively engaging youth, Benard points out, alienation is reduced. This plays a crucial role, as we have seen, in reducing other risk factors from teen pregnancy and dropping out of school to suicide and violent acting out. Specific opportunities to participate in meaningful activities include problem-solving, decision-making, planning, goal-setting, and helping others, according to Benard.

An excellent way to incorporate all of these activities is cooperative learning, which is rapidly being adopted by schools as a significant element in their restructuring efforts. Cooperative learning, with its emphasis on cooperation, group and individual goal-setting and problem-solving, leadership sharing and development, dialog and empathy, is tailor-made for preparing today's children for the increasingly complex world they will enter in the near future.

Various researchers cited by Benard tell us that schools can and often do operate in a manner that provides a protective shield for their student. In many cases, this form of operation exists in spite of adverse political and social climates in the educational community.

In her conclusion, Bonnie Benard reflects on the fact that all three of the above protective factors can be carried out in all systems by furthering our use of three "strategies of reciprocity." The strategies are: cooperative learning, peer helping, and mentoring. We must build the linkages between these systems, she insists, in order to restore the protective web that ultimately creates positive youth development.

In her concluding paragraphs, she states "while volumes can be written (and have!) on just how to go about this, the strategies are fairly simple and reflect not a need for behavioral interventions as much as for an *attitude change* [my emphasis]." I will return to the important role of attitude in the change process in the final section of this book.

All roads lead to Rome

As I think about what various researchers and writers are discovering about the nature of protective factors and resiliency, I am struck by a certain thematic connection from one to another. These themes seem to relate to what brain research and learning theory have to tell us about healthy childhood development. In the chart below we find a rough correlation between findings on learning theory, self-concept, asset building and resiliency as they all pertain to providing a protective environment for healthy childhood development.

In this chart, we begin with the findings of the Harvard researchers by assuming that learning is initiated by the stimulus of a model, followed by an opportunity to practice the behavior that was observed in the model, and then an opportunity to apply the modeled and practiced behavior in some meaningful way.

When Nancy Phillips talks about bonding, she is really talking about identification and involvement with a role model. Her discussions of a sense of control and the search for meaning correlate directly with the concept of practicing and applying the lessons learned during the bonding process.

Children gain a sense of control whenever they are provided with opportunities to be involved and derive a sense of meaning whenever they apply or contribute what they have learned in other areas of life.

In terms of the Benson research, support and care derive from the modeling and bonding opportunity. In monitoring and controlling the behavior of our youth, we create situations in which the young person can safely practice the skills they will need as adults. Within the framework of structured use of time, our youth can apply what they have learned in a positive, meaningful manner.

Research on Learning	Nancy Phillips	Peter Benson	Bonnie Benard
Stimulus from Model	Sense of bonding	Support and caring	Caring and support
Practice	Sense of control	Monitoring and control	High expectations
Application	Sense of meaning	Structured use of time	Involvement and participation

Figure 23: Correlates Between Learning Theory and Protective/Resiliency Factors

And finally, Bonnie Benard uses the terms care and support, high expectations, and opportunity for involvement and participation to describe the same aspects of positive youth development.

Thus, there appears to be a unified way of looking at a multitude of factors related to the well-being and healthy development of youth. What is emerging is a fundamental shift in our way of thinking about youth, their future and ours. This is the most hopeful paradigm shift that we have experienced in, roughly, the last twenty-five years. Two generations have been impacted by our pathology/deficit way of looking at the world. The next generations may be the ones to benefit from the new, more positive and hopeful, resiliency model.

Warnings!

Not all children bounce back. Where support is withdrawn or totally lacking, whether through shortsighted policy decisions, ignorance, or sheer neglect, we are going to have fewer and fewer children bouncing back. There is a growing concern among thoughtful people about certain policy makers and politicians who are using the case for resiliency as a way of arguing against providing support for some of the neediest portions of the population. There are those who will claim that we can reduce services because "kids bounce back anyway."

In the words of Neil Boothby, a Duke University professor and child psychologist who has studied children in war zones, "There is a danger among certain groups who advocate nonfederal involvement in assistance to children. They use it to blame people who don't move out of poverty. Internationally, the whole notion of resiliency has been used as an excuse not to do anything."[30]

Conservatives in particular, according to Lisbeth Schorr[31], a lecturer in social medicine at Harvard medical School, have argued against such proven interventions as Head Start and family support programs. Their argument is that "if these inner-city kids and families just showed a little grit they would pull themselves up by their own bootstraps." But, Schorr points out, " . . . those who study the dynamics of resilience say it matters little what is intrinsic to the child because the environment is so completely overwhelming." These researchers provide a sobering assessment about the limits of resilience when it comes to multiple-risk children—those facing not only poverty, but large families, absent fathers, drug-ridden neighborhoods, ineffective schools, and so forth. Simply stated, the more risk factors the worse the outcome. Short of changing the entire circumstance of these children, there is little reason to expect any of them to do well, according to Schorr. As a society, we are paying and we will continue to pay the price for these circumstances.

The challenge for the 1990's is to recognize that many of the neediest kids lack support at home, in school, or in the community. They cannot bounce back unless there are programs and people to supply the care and support that they are missing.

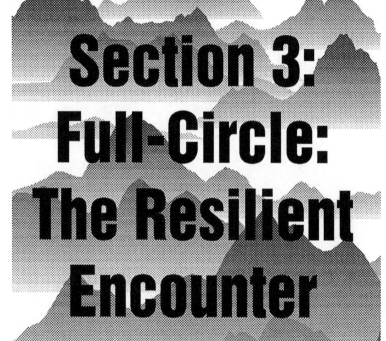

Section 3:
Full-Circle:
The Resilient
Encounter

Chapter 8: The Resilient Care Provider

Introduction

In this section, we will examine the basis of well-being and its importance to those of us committed to promoting positive youth development. Particular attention is paid to the role of belief and attitude in health and in our ability to make a difference with young persons—keeping in mind the central role played by belief and attitude that we learned about in the field of psychoneuroimmunology. We will also look at a proven method for reducing stress and maximizing overall health and well-being. By incorporating these ideas and practices into our lives, we can improve our own quality of life while providing a healthy model for the young persons with whom we live and work. As the expression goes, "unless we model what we teach, we are teaching something else."

If we are intent upon providing greater resilience in our children, then we, as care providers, must be mindful of what it is to be resilient. More than that, we must *live* in a resilient way.

In order to provide protective factors for children and provide a resilient shield, it is *necessary* to be knowledgeable and informed, although it isn't *sufficient*. Learning principles, as we discovered, emphasize how critical it is to provide access to the model. It follows that children will grow in health and resilience only as we, the adult care providers, identify, appreciate, and indeed demonstrate our own resiliency.

When queried about how he was able to peacefully bring about an end to British rule in India, Mahatma Ghandi answered very simply: "We must be the change we wish to see in the world." If we wish to bring forth a generation of healthy and resilient children, we, as adults, must show the way. In this, the final section of the book, we come full-circle. To accomplish our aim of fostering resilient children, *we must first foster resilience in ourselves*.

Attitude Adjustment

In his book, *The Seven Habits of Highly Effective People*, Stephen Covey[32] makes an intriguing observation about what might be considered the first habit that bodes well for success in life. It is the capacity to be more proactive than reactive in the face of life's events, challenges, opportunities, and dangers. He frames his discussion by using two circles, one inside the other. Outside of these circles are all the things occurring in our world, about which we feel no sense of concern—either because we are not aware of them or simply because we do not care. The larger circle contains what Covey calls our "Circle of Concern." The inner (smaller) circle is our "Circle of Influence."

According to Covey, we are being reactive whenever we put too much of our attention and energy on those concerns which, by definition, we can do little or nothing about.

Covey points out that this reactive focus actually reduces or shrinks our sphere of influence because our feelings of despair and powerlessness waste precious energy.

On the other hand, when we work mainly within our sphere of influence, we generate feelings associated with empowerment, efficacy, and success. These feelings, derived from a positive focus, actively enable us to expand our sphere of influence, both because of our success and because of our increased reservoir of positive energy.

Covey's articulation of a fundamental factor related to successful living reminds me of the teachings contained in the Serenity Prayer:

> *God, grant me the serenity*
> *to accept the things I cannot change,*
> *the courage to change*
> *the things I can*
> *And the wisdom*
> *to know the difference.*

Central to our sphere of influence— at the very center of the Circle of Influence—is attitude.

It is our attitude, properly cultivated and maintained, that ultimately determines our ability to make a difference, and to become effective agents of change .

Dr. William Carmack, professor of Social Policy and Community Development, said it so well: "Eighty-five percent of all successful change is due to the attitude of the change agent."

Bonnie Benard[33], reflecting on what the research indicates about successful change—as it relates to planned social change and resilient youth—outlines several principles essential to the change process. The very first one is the belief in our ability to make a difference. "Your belief in your ability to make a difference is the *sine qua non* for any change effort as well as a key trait of individual resiliency—it is what keeps a person going in the face of adversity."

The importance of attitude, as we learned from our exploration of psychoneuroimmunology, is being increasingly established as a key to reduced stress and enhanced wellness.

In fact, a most interesting medical discovery concerning the so-called "placebo" effect gives the importance of attitude an even firmer foundation. According to medical science, approximately thirty percent of those given a placebo respond positively—that is, their ache, pain, or complaint goes away. How is this possible? It is possible because of their *belief* that it will help.

It is due to an interpretation of an event which basically says: "This is going to help me in this way." Indeed, medical practitioners now speak of a "*nocebo*" effect which is the opposite of the placebo effect. It refers to those patients who are administered an actual medicine or drug—known to be an effective remedy—but are told that it is a placebo. Once again, about thirty percent have no reaction whatsoever to the compound they take.

Keeping this in mind, let us look further at how stress debilitates health and at the specific kinds of beliefs, attitudes, and behaviors that serve to minimize or even eliminate the negative impact of stress.

Psychological Hardiness and Well-being

Dr. Suzanne Kosaba[34], a wellness researcher at the University of Chicago, carried out an intriguing investigation into the role of attitude in stress reduction. In studies cited by Kosaba from psychoneuroimmunology, she describes the link between prolonged stress and greater instances of sickness.

One way to look at how prolonged stress can lead to illness is to study Figure 24.

The human body is well equipped to deal with acute stress. Our autonomic nervous system and neuroendocrine system respond to threats (either real or perceived) in the "fight or flight" fashion, by producing elevated levels of adrenal steroids and cortisols. If we cope effectively, we essentially return to normal over time. The amount of time it takes to return to a normal state is governed by many factors such as our overall health, interpretation of events, diet, and exercise.

Returning to the diagram in Figure 24, the direct effects of stress are related to changes or alterations occurring in our nervous and endocrine systems. The indirect effects of stress are related to behaviors that we do in response to our perceptions of threat. These behaviors include over-eating, under-eating, poor diet choices, smoking, drinking, or drug use, etc.

Taken together and prolonged over time, the direct and indirect effects of stress alter our immune system's ability to function in a normal and healthy manner. Basically, the elevated levels of cortisol and steroids interfere with the body's first line of defense—the formation of healthy white blood cells. When these monocytes and leucocytes develop poorly or in insufficient numbers, we are left open to infections, allergies, some forms of cancer, and other diseases of an auto-immunity nature.

Thus, Dr. Kosaba—after citing some of the studies related to the reduction of health and increased sickness associated with prolonged stress—goes on to describe a landmark finding in the study of stress. This was a study carried out in late 1970 by Dr. Arron Antonopsky.

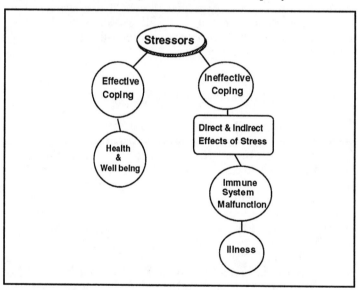

Figure 24: Stress and Well-being

At that time, the Supreme Court passed down a decision that the Bell Telephone Company could no longer operate as a monopoly, and would have to break up into smaller operating units to allow competition. Dr. Antonopsky saw this as a unique opportunity to study the effects of a prolonged stressful readjustment on the lives of some 400 carefully selected managers.

He used two comparison groups consisting of approximately 200 managers each. In one group were those who exhibited three behaviors and/or attitudes correlated with effective coping. These included:

- exercising three to four times per week

- belief that they were well supported by their own superiors

- psychological hardiness

The benefits of exercise as a tactic to effectively reduce stress levels is well documented. It is, perhaps, the most efficient method we know to help metabolize and rid the body of the accumulation of stress-related hormones. The element of support is a consistent theme in nearly all research related to stress and well-being. The concept of psychological hardiness will be described a bit later in this chapter.

The other group exhibited none of the three behaviors and attitudes associated with effective coping.

Not surprisingly—but of the utmost importance to those conducting this ground-breaking research—those in the first group accounted for very little of the sickness observed during the long period of time when stresses built up and intensified. In fact, those who regularly exercised, perceived the workplace as a supportive environment, and displayed psychological hardiness, accounted for less that seven percent of the sickness in the combined groups of 400.

Members of the second group accounted for the other ninety-three percent of the illnesses during the time-frame of the study.

Dr. Kosaba's contribution was related to her interest in which, if any, of the three factors is more important than the others in maintaining health in the face of stress. She discovered that psychological hardiness was the greatest determinant of health and wellness. Interestingly enough, psychological hardiness consists of three factors, each of which is attitudinal in nature.

The Three Cs of Psychological Hardiness

The first factor is how we respond to *challenge*. A key feature of psychological hardiness is the belief that life's changes can be an impetus or stimulus for personal growth instead of a threat to the *status quo*. It comes down to seeing challenge as an opportunity to make a difference.

Challenge, control, and commitment are the key ingredients of psychological hardiness, and may well be the most essential basis of well-being, vitality, and health in the face of chronic stress

The next factor is *control*. It is the opposite of helplessness. Here we have the attitude or belief that we can influence events coupled with the willingness to act on that belief rather than becoming a victim of circumstances. Covey called this sense of control the Circle of Influence. Again, I am reminded of the Serenity Prayer, which has served as an ideal for all who are learning the power of letting go of what is beyond our control, on the one hand, and taking courageous action, on the other.

The third factor is *commitment*. Commitment entails the decision to act based upon an attitude of curiosity and involvement in whatever is happening in our sphere of influence. It involves the decision to go through the highs and lows associated with following a particular vision, dream, calling, or task. Its opposite, interestingly enough, is alienation.

Challenge, control, and commitment are the key ingredients of psychological hardiness, and may well be the most essential basis of well-being, vitality, and health in the face of chronic stress. Most importantly, each is within our ability to grasp because they are related to our *perceptions* of events, and our attitudes towards those events. Our attitude is at the center of our sphere of influence and relates both directly and indirectly to our quality of life and health.

Chapter 9: A Context for Resiliency

At this point, I want to explore what I think is the broadest context of psychological hardiness and resilience—a purposive life.

I once heard it said that the purpose of our lives is threefold:

- finding our way to God

- healing our wounds

- expressing our gifts

This, to me, is such a clear explanation of life's purpose. In thinking about it, I have become aware of how well it serves as a blueprint for a meaningful life.

In a very personal way, it encouraged me by affirming three of life's most compelling and important features. It validated the difficult but liberating work of healing that so many of us have chosen to do in order to grow. This work includes giving up our destructive patterns of denial and compulsion while working through the stages of grief related to loss, letting go, and moving on. It also affirmed my deeply-felt need to continue to discover and develop my gifts. To me, there is no greater joy than to share in and pass along the benefits of these combined efforts.

This triad of facing and working through our pain and expressing our joy, in the context of a true connection with the God of our understanding, aids greatly in the imperative to find meaning in our lives. It embraces so much of what ails and concerns us, motivates and drives us, and deepens and connects us. As such, it is an excellent map or blueprint for a coherent life.

The pathology-deficiency model, at its best, embraced one aspect of this triad (often to the exclusion of the other two)—healing our wounds. The resiliency model encourages us to look at what makes us flexible, adaptable, and strong, often despite adversity and the hard knocks of life. Inspired by a sincere and heart-felt spiritual connection, we have a potent and balanced way of living fully in the midst of raising and working with children and young people.

In her synthesis of findings on what it takes to foster resiliency in children, Bonnie Benard maintained that a most important characteristic was a strong sense of purpose and a positive sense of the future. I would like to examine further this notion of our own purpose, expanding upon the trinitarian format that I just mentioned.

The first component of purpose is deepening our connection with God. I think again of the practical definition of *spirituality* that H. Steven Glenn provides. Glenn says that spirituality is an active identification with a power greater than ourselves that gives our lives a sense of meaning and purpose. I think the word religion would work just as well if we were to use its original meaning: to *reconnect*. This is precisely what is meant by finding our way to a God of our understanding.

It seems to be very much a part of our biological nature to find meaning through our connections. When we connect with something—a person, nature, community, God—we become involved or identified with it. Through this active involvement, we derive a sense of belonging, of significance, and of importance. Furthermore, it appears to matter not whether that connection is fulfilling and positive or degrading and destructive. A gang will, unfortunately, fill in for a family. Connecting with a James Jones or David Koresh can result in losing one's life, instead of adding to it.

The challenge that each of us faces, is how to fulfill a need, that is sometimes felt as a yearning or, perhaps, a vague dissatisfaction with our lives. It is my own belief that each of us is born with a "spark of the spirit" and it is our task to ignite it into a living flame. All true religions have proffered a path or method for igniting this flame.

This brings us to the second aspect of our greater purpose: healing our wounds.

We live in an imperfect world. None of us gets all of our needs met (and here I am speaking about real needs—love, belonging, someone to hear our story, along with basic material needs).

It is my own belief that each of us is born with a "spark of the spirit" and it is our task to ignite it into a living flame. All true religions have proffered a path or method for igniting this flame.

Some of us are fortunate enough to have most needs met, while others have few. Those who have too few, of course, fail to thrive or, indeed, survive. So it is that we all, to one degree or another, become wounded. Our hurts and psychic wounds can be real or imagined—it doesn't matter which. This is life—not always fair, but ultimately, just.

In many ways and when properly and ethically applied, the pathology model can serve us well while dealing with the problem of psychic wounds. There are many caring and skilled therapists and helping professionals as well as books that can assist us in freeing ourselves from the painful burden of past wounds. This can liberate our energies for more positive endeavors, pursuits, and relationships as surely as can those other aspects of our purpose—connecting with God and expressing our gifts.

The third aspect of purpose is to find and express our gifts. It is undeniable that all of us have at least one gift to nurture, develop, and bring into the world. Dr. Howard Gardner[35] of Yale University has set forth the claim, difficult to dispute, that everyone of us is gifted in at least one area of intelligence. His landmark research on what he discovered to be seven discrete forms of intelligence (spatial, body-kinesthetic, musical, mathematical-logical, linguistic, interpersonal, and intrapersonal) provides a refreshing acknowledgment of the creative capacity that is the birthright of each of us.

Ultimately, I believe we can expect a greater and more widespread acceptance of this finding. One hopes it will ease the way for policies and programs that encourage the development of these gifts in our children. In the meantime, we can all rest assured that we do indeed have at least one major gift.

Perhaps the easiest way of finding what our gifts are is to list those activities that provide us with the most joy and fulfillment when we do them. Usually, our passions in life are closely related to our gifts. To discover potential gifts, those that may be dormant and as yet untapped, a useful exercise is to make a list of our dreams. What is it that we dream or fantasize about being or doing or having? By following this lead, by pursuing our dream or dreams, we can find and claim our gifts.

Enhancing Our Own Resistance to Stress

Fortunately for us, there is one important proactive behavior that we can incorporate into our often hectic lifestyles; one that has been proven to bring about significant benefits to the lives of those who practice it. It is a practical method by which we can augment our psychological and physical hardiness.

In 1975, Dr. Herbert Benson[36], with the Harvard Medical School, authored a national best-seller. The book, *The Relaxation Response*, chronicles his ground-breaking research on patients in his stress-reduction laboratory. Since that time, many thousands of patients have benefited from his clinic and tens of thousands of those who have read his book (or his two more recent books on the same topic) and practiced the technique have benefited accordingly.

As background to this rather remarkable health enhancing technique, let us review, one last time, the link between brain, mind, and spirit.

Stress and the Brain

Certain areas of the brain are sites for our anxiety-provoked or threat-provoked reactions. These threats can be either real or imagined. In fact, an axiom of the stress field is that ninety percent of all stress is perceptual. The only constants—consistently threatening to all of us—are things like loud noise and other noxious environmentally induced stressors. These make up about ten percent of the total stressors we experience, according to this line of thinking.

It is generally agreed that the degree of stress that we experience is directly related to our *interpretation* of events. What is interpreted as threatening to one person isn't necessarily true for the next. For example, being asked to give a public speech might fill one individual with sheer terror while another may feel an exhilarating sense of anticipation and excitement. The difference between these diametrically opposed reactions also have very different effects on the body, of course.

The link between our perceptions, the interpretation of those perceptions, and the findings about psychological hardiness are strong. Our attitudes or beliefs derive from our perception of events. Depending on how we ultimately *choose* to respond— no matter how small, narrow, or limited the choice appears to be—we gain or lose in health and well-being.

Our brain responds immediately to our interpretation of events. In the case of a perceived threat to our well-being, the sympathetic nervous system is aroused. The more frequently this fight-or-flight mechanism is aroused, the more sensitized it becomes. This was one of Benson's key findings. The greater the degree of arousal and the frequency with which that arousal occurs, the more sensitized those areas of the brain become. This neurologic hyper-sensitivity, according to Benson, may involve a process known as "kindling" in brain tissues. Kindling refers to a process whereby parts of the brain become overly sensitized due to repeated stimulation and arousal. In time, these areas of the brain respond to *less* stimulation while simultaneously responding more powerfully to normal stimuli. In this manner, stress induces greater and greater levels of "fight or flight" reactions in the brain.

When this hyper-arousal or kindling occurs, the body, of course, is also involved. In this case, the body revs up and releases the adrenal steroids and cortisols (mentioned ear-

---

Kindling refers to a process whereby parts of the brain become overly sensitized due to repeated stimulation and arousal. In time, these areas of the brain respond to less *stimulation while simultaneously responding more powerfully to normal stimuli. In this manner, stress induces greater and greater levels of "fight or flight" reactions in the brain.*

---

lier), which make us tense, irritable, and distractible. This tension also affects our ability to concentrate or focus. Because the ancient or lower brain is in control, our higher mental processes or capabilities are pushed into the background. In this situation, we react to events impulsively, and perhaps with future regret, instead of thoughtfully considering the consequences ahead of time.

In addition, the neuropeptides and neurohormones involved in thought affect our emotions, which, in turn, affect our monocytes, or white blood cells—that first line of immune defense. Of course, when our emotions are impacted by stress, we are also more prone to defensiveness and inappropriate emotional responses.

Since the brain, body, thought, and emotions are all interconnected, it is easy to see how a negative feedback loop can begin and create a downward spiral. The results of this downward spiral can, in the end, rob us of our peace of mind, serenity, productivity, and eventually our health. It is easy to understand, in today's society, how stress-related illnesses account for eighty percent of all medical problems.

What, then, is one to do?

The Relaxation Response

Dr. Benson taught his patients a very simple technique that proved to be very successful in nearly all cases. His books cite numerous instances in which patients made dramatic improvements and gains, not only in health, but also in the areas of careers, life goals, and relationships, when they practiced the "relaxation response."

What is most interesting and important is what Dr. Benson and his investigating team of scientists discovered in their studies. Before summarizing those landmark findings, I would like to briefly describe the relaxation response. For a fuller and more detailed explanation of the process, I encourage the interested reader to learn, and above all, *practice* this remarkable technique. (See the bibliography for a list of Dr. Benson's books.)

Learning to Relax

A very simple procedure indeed, the most difficult part of the relaxation response is to actually *do it*—consistently and over time. What it amounts to is choosing a quiet place and time (it is best to do it the same time each day) in which to sit with eyes closed, and focus on the rhythm of one's breath as it enters and leaves the body. The idea is to focus completely on the breath as it goes in and out, counting from one to ten and then repeating. As the mind begins to wander, which it inevitably will do, one gently brings it back to the counting. Benson discovered that the procedure can create even more remarkable results if one uses a word, phrase, or image tied to a deeply held value or belief. Often this is of a religious nature, involving an image of an object of worship, a mantra, or a prayer.

The image or word is seen or quietly spoken on each outward breath. By doing this simple practice one to two times each day, for ten to twenty minutes each time, truly remarkable benefits can be achieved, according to Dr. Benson's team of researchers.

By totally relaxing in a mindful and conscious way, the body undergoes subtle but profound changes, especially when done in a consistent manner over time. Dr. Benson claims that twenty minutes spent doing the relaxation response is the equivalent in benefit to the brain and body of several hours of sleep. Other researchers are reporting that it may actually extend the length of one's lifetime. Obviously, relaxation has a most salutary effect upon the nervous system, because it is the parasympathetic nervous system that is being brought into play.

This aspect of our nervous system is designed to counter the potentially harmful effect of frequent arousal of the sympathetic nervous system—the fight or flight, adrenalin-activated mechanism associated with stress.

Consciously learning to activate the parasympathetic nervous system, Benson points out, actually begins to "dekindle" the brain. The brain, over time, becomes less and less prone to overreactivity and eventually becomes, in a sense, programmed not to react in such harmful ways to stress (or to our interpretation of events as stressful).

The Proven Benefits of Relaxation

Over the years that the Harvard medical school investigated the salutary effects of deep relaxation, some very amazing benefits were discovered. Benson lists four items of paramount significance to health and overall well-being.

1. Increased hemispheric communication in the brain.

Both halves of the brain, when they communicate efficiently with each other, work in a balanced and effective manner. It is easy to "overwork" one hemisphere, for example, working long hours in front of a computer—more of a left-brain effort. This can lead to tiredness and inefficiency. Utilizing the relaxation response "tunes" both hemispheres, leading to increased communication between them, resulting in enhanced productivity.

2. Transformation of brain cells, and establishment of new nerve pathways.

Amazingly enough, these scientists were able to show evidence of actual neurological changes in the brain when patients learned how to activate the relaxation response on a regular basis. Whenever the brain changes, ability changes—in this case for the better.

3. The role of belief in triggering changes in the mind, body, and immune system is now firmly established.

The evidence for neurological changes and enhanced hemispheric communication emphasizes the role of our attitudes in creating (or destroying) health. While this is not yet universally accepted, it is becoming harder to dispute it on scientific grounds.

4. The relaxation response plays a crucial role in life-transforming changes.

Dr. Benson's books are filled with case-study examples of people whose health, relationships, careers, and even spiritual life were improved by the regular practice of relaxation. Some of those changes were quite profound.

I will leave it to the interested reader to discover the details of these hopeful and encouraging discoveries. I found Dr. Benson's books to be based on good science, easy to read and inspirational, as well.

As care-givers intent on fostering resiliency in children and young people, it is essential that we recognize, affirm, and foster our own resiliency. Learning to control and offset the effects of stress while we simultaneously enhance our hardiness and resilience helps us to effectively use the most important learning tool children and young people can ever have—ourselves.

Epilogue

Epilogue

At the beginning of the book we highlighted the nature of societal change and its impact on the family. It was stressed that the Baby Boomers experienced an historically unprecedented number of deficits in their lives. In particular, the lack of bonding and connectedness to family, school, and community, combined with a high degree of passivity in the face of classroom practices and television watching had precipitated a "generation at-risk." The result, it was noted, was that Baby Boomers would grow up to become the most drug-affected and divorced generation in American history. Viewed through the lens of the pathology/deficit paradigm, we would conclude that this was the most dysfunctional generation ever.

Furthermore, we don't even have to speculate on what effect that dysfunction would bring to bear on the succeeding generations. The evidence is clear—today's teens and pre-teens are displaying the greatly magnified symptoms of increased distress and disconnectedness, as any number of statistics and trends attest.

And now we have the arrival of the grandchildren of the Baby Boomers in our schools. What, we are well advised to ask, is their fate?

Since our actions are, in large measure, related to our beliefs and attitudes, and since our attitudes are shaped and fashioned by our viewpoints, let us re-examine today's parents from a different vantage point. While the pathology/deficit view is accurate and useful, it does not represent the entire picture of Baby

Boomers. For, in addition to having certain deficits that played a clear role in their troubles, the Baby Boomer generation also became the most activist, idealistic, and socially involved generation as they entered the young adult years.

By identifying themselves with a power greater than themselves—whether it was social justice, environmental protection, or ending an ugly and morally unjust war—many, if not most, Baby Boomers were attempting to create a better world while deriving a sense of connectedness, meaning, and significance—all of which relate to our earlier definition of spirituality.

To say that the Baby Boom generation was "spirited" as young adults would be an understatement, of course. Easier to miss, is the fact that, as a generation, they were also acting in a spiritual manner, although it was often confused, misguided, and not without negative and even dire consequences. The point is that if spirituality can be defined as an identification or involvement with a power greater than ourselves that gives life a sense of purpose and meaning, then Baby Boomers, by and large, were involved in a profoundly spiritual quest.

The sobering fact of life that sooner of later had to be faced, however, was that changing our institutions is a slow and daunting process. At the same time, the realities of having to raise children, earn an income, and, eventually, becoming senior citizens, would mean a reduction of youthful idealism and activism.

The challenge that we now face is how to tap this reservoir of idealism and social activism that once spilled over into excess and youthful exuberance. How can we use what was unique to much of an entire generation again, but in a different manner and for succeeding generations whose very future depends upon our attitudes and action?

In his book, *Childhood's Future*[37], Richard Louv provides an insight into this urgent question, framing it in a developmental context. It is not, he points out, just children who have developmental needs that must be met. We, as adults, have them as well. The developmental imperative for Baby Boom parents is to operate in the stage of Eriksonian development called *generativity*.

Erikson described it as a time in which generativity or stagnation holds sway in the lives of those roughly in their forties. For those with children, the term generativity takes on the decided undertone of *generations* or *generational*. In this context, it refers to care of the next generation.

Louv points out that it isn't just that children need their parents and other adults. As adults, we need to be needed by our children. Louv is talking about *meaning* which underlies the magical importance of modeling, mirroring, and bonding. It works both ways. Children and adults alike are at-risk today because of the lack of positive contact between them.

It is hoped that the recognition of our need to be needed by our own children, and all of society's children will spur us to close the gap and increase the amount of positive contact between the generations. It isn't just for our children and their future that we must do it. It is for the well-being—developmentally, socially, economically, emotionally, and spiritually—of all of us, now and in the future, that we must strive.

Taken to heart, we cannot but win this battle for our children and our future. May we, together, and in a spirit of hope and optimism, move from risk to resilience.

Notes

Notes

[1]   Bronfenbrenner, Urie. Feb. 1986. "Alienation and the Four Worlds of Children." *Phi Delta Kappan,* pp 430-436.

[2]   Benson, Peter. 1990. "The Troubled Journey: A Portrait of American Youth." Search Institute. 700 South Third St. Suite 210. Minneapolis, MN.

[3] Louv, Richard. 1987. *Childhood's Future: Listening to the American Family—Hope and Solutions for the Next Generation.* Doubleday, New York.

[4] Glenn, H. Stephen. 1989. *Raising Self-Reliant Children in a Self-Indulgent World.* Sunrise Press, Fairoaks, CA.

[5] Phillips, Nancy. July, 1990. "Wellness During Adolescent Development." *Prevention Forum,* Vol. 10, No. 4. Phillips points out that positive self-concept is correlated highly with overall well being in every area except the use of alcohol. To me, this is a sad commentary on the modeling in contemporary society. In this case, advertising is a most significant model for the use of alcohol, and a primary advertising target is young people. The power of modeling in human bonding, learning, and behavior will be dealt with later in the chapter. So powerful is media modeling that despite significant efforts to reduce teen drinking, there has been little progress in the past two decades. In fact, numerous surveys indicate that the problem is worsening.

[6] Pearce, Joseph Chilton. 1992. *Evolution's End: Claiming the Potential of Our Intelligence.* Harper-Collins, San Francisco, CA.

In my mind, this is the most important book written on childhood development and the potential that is inherent in every human being at birth. Pearce has synthesized an enormous amount of scientific data to support his contentions and conclusions. See also his earlier book, *The Magical Child Matures.* Bantam Books, 1986.

[7] Peck, Scott. 1978. *The Road Less Traveled.* Touchstone Books, New York.

[8] Healy, Jane M. 1990. *Endangered Minds: Why Children Don't Think and What We Can Do About It.* Touchstone Books, New York.

Much of what follows in this part of the book comes from Healy's discoveries about the developing brain. In addition, the role of myelin in brain maturation and learning can be found in the writings of Joseph Chilton Pearce. See also, "Myelin and Maturation: A Fresh Look at Piaget." Virginia R. Johnson, *The Science Teacher.* Vol. 49, No. 3, March, 1982.

[9] Robertson, Joel C. June/July 1989. "Changing Self-Destructive Behavior in Adolescents Through Recreational Activities." *Adolescent Counselor.*

[10] Borysenko, Joan. 1988. *Minding the Body, Mending the Mind,* Bantnam Books, New York.

[11] Seligman, Martin E. P. 1990. *Learned Optimism: How to Change Your Mind and Your Life.* Pocket Books, New York. For anyone with an interest in the roots of depression—currently at epidemic levels in our society—this is must reading.

[12] Werner, Emmy. April, 1989. "Children of the Garden Island." *Scientific American.* pp 106-111.

[13] Rutter, Michael. March 1984. "Resilient Children. *Psychology Today,* pp 57-65.and Rutter, Michael. 1985. "Resilience in the Face of Adversity: Protective Factors and Resistance to Psychiatric Disorder." *British Journal of Psychiatry,* Volume 147, pp 598-611.

[14] Garmezy, Norman. March/April, 1991. "Resilience and Vulnerability to Adverse Developmental Outcomes Associated with Poverty." *American Behavioral Scientist*, Volume 34, Number 4.

See *Resilience Among High Risk Youth*, listed in the bibiography. This work is a succinct, yet comprehensive overview of the interface between the risk and the resilience constructs.

[15] Beardslee, William R. July 1983. "Children of Parents with Major Affective Disorders: A Review." *American Jounal of Psychiatry*, Volume 140, pp 825-832.

[16] Beardslee, William R. and Podorefsky, Donna. January, 1988. "Resilient Adolescents Whose Parents Have Serious Affective and Other Psychiatric Disorders: The Importance of Self-Understanding and Relationships." *American Journal of Psychiatry*, Volume 145, Number 1.

[17] Segal, Julius. 1986. *Winning Life's Toughest Battles: Roots of Human Resilience*. McGraw-Hill, New York.

[18] Seligman, *Learned Optimism*.

[19] Hawkins, David J., Catalano, Richard F., Miller, Janey Y. 1992. "Risk and Protective Factors for Alcohol and Other Drug Problems in Adolescence and Early Adulthood: Implications for Substance-abuse Programs." *Psychological Bulletin*. Volume 112, Number 1.

[20] Benson. "The Troubled Journey."

[21] Pittman, Karen J. September 30, 1991. "A New Vision: Promoting Youth Development." Testimony provided to the Congressional House Select Committee of Children, Youth and Family.

[22] Beardslee. "Children of Parents With Major Affective Disorders."

[23] Miller, Alice. 1990. *The Untouched Key: Tracing Childhood Trauma in Creativity and Destructiveness*. Doubleday, New York.

[24] Bronfenbrenner, Urie. As quoted in Benard, Bonnie. 1990. "Fostering Resiliency in Kids: Protective Factors in the Family, School and Community."

[25] Richardson, Glenn E., et al. Nov/Dec 1990. "The Resiliency Model." *Health Education.*

[26] Benard, Bonnie. 1991 "Fostering Resiliency in Kids: Protective Factors in the Family, School and Community" Western Regional Center for Drug-Free Schools and Communities, Far West Laborator. San Francisco, CA.

[27] Benard, Bonnie. "Fostering Resiliency...". page 10.

[28] Benard, Bonnie. "Fostering Resiliency...". page 11.

[29] Benard, Bonnie. "Fostering Resiliency...". page 12.

[30] Boothby, Neil. Summer 1991. As quoted in "The Miracle of Resiliency." David Gelman. *Newsweek.* Volume 117, Number 1.

[31] Schorr, Lisbeth. As quoted in "The Miracle of Resiliency." by David Gelman. *Newsweek.* Volume 117, Number 1.

[32] Covey, Stephen R. 1989. *The Seven Habits of Highly Effective People.* Simon and Schuster. New York.

[33] Benard, Bonnie. March 1992. "Creating Change Requires Vision and Interaction." *Western Center News.* Far West Laboratory, Drug-Free Schools and Communities. San Francisco, CA.

[34] Kosaba, Suzanne, et al. 1985. "Effectiveness of Hardiness, Exercise and Social Support as Resources Against Illness." *Journal of Psychosomatic Research.* Volume 29, Number 5.

[35] Gardner, Howard. 1983. *Frames of Mind: The Theory of Multiple Intelligences.* Basic Books, Inc. New York.

[36] Benson, Herbert. 1975. *The Relaxation Response.* Avon Books. New York.

[37] Louv, Richard. *Childhood's Future.*

Appendix A
External and Internal Assets

External Assets as Defined in the Troubled Journey, by Peter Benson

Asset Type	Asset Name	Asset Definition
Support	1. Family support	Family life provides high levels of love and support
	2. Parent(s) as social resources	Student views parent(s) as accessible resources for advice and support
	3. Parent communication	Student has frequent, in-depth conversations with parent(s)
	4. Other adult resources	Student has access to non-parent adults for advice and support
	5. Other adult communication	Student has frequent, in-depth conversations with non-parent adults
	6. Parent involvement in schooling	Parent(s) are involved i helping student succeed in school
	7. Positive school climate	School provides a caring, encouraging environment
Control	8. Parental standards	Parent(s) have standards for appropriate conduct
	9. Parental discipline	Parent(s) discipline student when a rule is violated
	10. Parental monitoring	Parent(s) monitor "where am I going and with whom I will be"
	11. Time at home	Student goes out for "fun and recreation" 3 or fewer nights per week
	12. Positive peer influence	Student's best friends model responsible behavior
Structured Time Use	13. Involved in music	Student spends 1 hour or more per week in music training or practice
	14. Involved in school extra-curricular activities	Student spends 1 hour of more per week in school sports, clubs, or arganizations
	15. Involved in community organizations or activities	Student spends 1 hour or more per week in organization or clubs outside of school
	16. Involved in church or synagogue	Student spends 1 hour or more per wekk attending programs or services

Internal Assets as Defined in the Troubled Journey, by Peter Benson

Asset Type	Asset Name	Asset Definition
Educational Commitment	1. Achievement motivation	Student is motivated to do well in school
	2. Educational aspiration	Student aspires to pursue post-high school education (trade school, college)
	3. School performance	Student reports school performance in above average
	4. Homework	Student reports 6 hours or more of homework per week
Positive Values	5. Values helping people	Student places high personal value on helping other people
	6. In concerned about world hunger	Student reports interest in helping to reduce world hunger
	7. Cares about people's feelings	Student cares about other people's feelings
	8. Value sexual restraint	Sutdent values postponing sexual activity
Social Competence	9. Assertiveness skills	Student reports ability to "stand up for what I believe"
	10. Decision-making skills	Student reports "I am good at making decisions"
	11. Friendship-making skills	Student reports "I am good at makig friends"
	12. Planning skills	Student reports "I am good at planning"
	13. Self-esteem	Student reports high self-esteem
	14. Positive view of personal future	Student is optimistic about his/her personal future

Appendix B
Risk Indicators

Risk Indicators, as Presented in *The Troubled Journey*, by Peter Benson.

At-risk Domain	At-risk Indicator	Definition	Total Youth
Alcohol	1. Frequent alcohol use	Has used alcohol 6 or more times "in the last 30 days"	11%
	2. Binge dringing	Has had 5 or more drinks in a row, once or more "in the last 2 weeks"	23%
Tobacco	3. Daily cigarette use	Smoke 1 or more cigarettes per day	12%
	4. Frequent chewing tobacco use	Has used 20 or more times "in the last 12 months"	5%
Illicit Drugs	5. Frequent use of illicit drugs	Has used marijuana, cocaine or crack, PCP, LSD, amphetamines, heroin, or other narcotics 6 or more times "in the last 12 months"	8%
Sexuality	6. Sexually active	Has had sexual intercourse 2 or more times	30%
	7. Non-use of contraceptives	Is sexually active, and self or partner does not always use contraceptives	47%
Depression/ Suicide	8. Depression	Is sad or depressed "most of the time" or "all of the time"	15%
	9. Attempted suicide	Has attempted suicide once or more	13%
Anti-social Behavior	10. Vandalism	Destroyed property "just for fun," 2 or more times "in the last 12 months"	10%
	11. Group fighting	Took part in a fight between two groups or gangs, 2 or more times "in the last 12 months"	13%
	12. Police trouble	Got into trouble with the police, 2 or more times "in the last 12 months'	7%
	13. Theft	Stole something from a store, 2 or more times "in the last 12 months"	10%
	14. Weapon use	Used knife, gun, or other weapon "to get something from a person," 2 or more times "in the last 12 months"	2%
School problems	15. School absenteeism	Skipped school 2 or more days "in the last month"	10%
	16. Desire to drop out	Wants to quit school before completing high school	1%
Vehicle Safety	17. Driving and Drinking	Has driven after drinking 2 or more times "in the last year"	11%
	18. Riding and Drinking	Has ridden with a driver who had been drinking 2 or more times "in the last year"	33%
	19. Seat belt non-use	Does not use seat belts "all" or "most" of the time	50%
Other	20. Bulimia	Vomits on purpose after eating, once a week or more	2%

Appendix C

Community Protective Factors

Community Protective Factors Recommended for Fostering Resilience

Risk Factors		Protective Factors
Individual and Peer	Family	
Early antisocial behavior	Lack of clear behavioral expectations	A relationship with a caring adult role model
Alienation and rebelliousness	Lack of monitoring and supervision	Opportunity to contribute and be seen as a resource
Antisocial behavior in later childhood and early teens	Lack of caring	Effectiveness in work, play, and relationships
Favorable attitudes toward drug use	Inconsistent or excessively severe discipline	Healthy expectations and positiveoutlook
Susceptibility to peer influence	Parental positive attitudes toward alcohol and other drug use	Self-esteem and internal locus-of-control
Freinds who use tobacco, alcohol or other drugs	Low expectations for children's success	Self-discipline
	History of alcohol and drug abuse	Problem solving/critical thinking skills
		A sense of humor

Recommendations for Parents

- Place high priority on expressing love and support to fulfill children's bonding needs

- Set clear rules and limits to provide the requirements for monitoring and control

- Encourage involvement in structured youth activities as a form of community involvement

- Minimize attendance at drinking parties

- Model responsible chemical use and vehicle safety behaviors

- Make "family helping" projects a priority

- Ensourage and reward achievement motivation

- Minimize exposure to TV and other mass media forms

- Emphasize the development of positive values

- Advocate for effective schools and community yourth-serving organization

Recommendations for Educators

- Personalize schools so that each and every child feels cared for

- Enhance social competencies and skills

- Emphasize the deveopment of positive values

- Offer quality prevention programs in multiple areas of risk

- Enhance academic effectiveness for students in all income levels

- Emphasize service learning programs

- Provide strong support services for youth at risk

Recommendations for Community Leaders

- Assemble a permanenet child and youth task force involving leaders from all community sectors

- Create a community-wide visison for youth development

- Continually assess progress toward the vision

- Create a detailed action plan to promote positive youth development

- Emphasize youth access to effective schools, families, and youth-serving organizations

- Advocate for greater state and federal support for school effectiveness, parent education, day care and after school care, prevention programming, and other efforts promoting positive youth development

- Ensure that one's community offers a range of support services for families and structured, adult-led activities for youth.

Protective Factors Within the Community

"The Competent Community"

Caring and Support

Social networks (intergenerational)

Social Cohesion/Fabric

Availability of Resources

(Healthcare, Childcare, Housing, Education, Job training, Employment, Recreation)

High Expectations

Youth viewed as Resources

Alcohol/Drug use norms

Valuing Youth

Opportunities for participation

Socially and economically useful tasks

Defined Roles

Engage!

Youth service

Appendix D

The Research of Nancy Phillips

The Research of Nancy Phillips

At this point, I would like to introduce the research of Nancy Phillips whose work analyzed "at-risk" factors and and protective factors that can be used to counteract risk factors.

This particular research was undertaken in an attempt to describe a single condition or a characteristic that—if possessed by young people —would allow them to face life in a low-risk mode. It was, in a sense, what we might call a protective factor search. What *one* factor might stand out above all others that would serve to reduce risk in young people? In her paper, Phillips describes one such factor that both common sense and much good research tell us will protect young people.

That one factor is positive self-concept. When self-concept is positive, we have a low-risk young person in every area except one. The one exception is the area of alcohol abuse, which says a great deal about the widespread acceptance of alcohol in our society. It also emphasizes a point that will be expanded in a later chapter: the importance of role modeling in human learning and development.

A sense of control, I mean my belief, as a growing human being, that I have the power and control to shape the forces that are trying to shape me. It is the conviction that I am in an interactive process exerting some direct control over what is happening in my life. It requires self-discipline.

A sense of bonding means that I have a sense of belonging in the major institutions that impact my life—my family, my school, my community.

My sense of meaning tells me that my life makes sense and that I feel significant and important.

Bibliography

Bibliography

Anthony, E. J. and Cohler, B. eds. 1987. *The Invulnerable Child*. Guilford Press. New York.

Beardslee, William R. July 1983. "Children of Parents with Major Affective Disorders: A Review." *American Jounal of Psychiatry*, Volume 140.

Beardslee, William R. and Podorefsky, Donna. January, 1988. "Resilient Adolescents Whose Parents Have Serious Affective and Other Psychiatric Disorders: The Importance of Self-Understanding and Relationships." *American Journal of Psychiatry*, Volume 145, Number 1.

Benard, Bonnie. January 1990. "Youth Serivce: From Youth as Problems to Youth as Resources." *Illinois Prevention Forum*. Volume 10, Number 1.

Benard, Bonnie. 1991 "Fostering Resiliency in Kids: Protective Factors in the Family, School and Community" Western Regional Center for Drug-Free Schools and Communities, Far West Laborator. San Francisco, CA.

Benard, Bonnie. March 1992. "Creating Change Requires Vision and Interaction." *Western Center News*. Far West laboratory, Drug-Free Schools and Communities. San Francisco, CA.

Benson, Herbert. 1975. *The Relaxation Response.* Avon Books. New York.

Benson, Herbert. 1987. *Your Maximum Mind.* Random House. New York.

Benson, Peter. 1990."The Troubled Journey: A Portrait of American Youth." Search Institute. 700 South Third St. Suite 210. Minneapolis, MN.

Boothby, Neil. Summer 1991. As quoted in "The Miracle of Resiliency." David Gelman. *Newsweek.* Volume 117, Number 1.

Borysenko, Joan. 1988. *Minding the Body, Mending the Mind,* Bantnam Books, New York.

Bronfenbrenner, Urie. Feb. 1986. "Alienation and the Four Worlds of Children." *Phi Delta Kappan.*

Bronfenbrenner, Urie. 1974. *The Ecology of Human Development.* Harvard University Press. Cambridge, MA.

Chopra, Deepak. 1989. *Quantam Healing: Exploring the Frontiers of Mind-Body Medicine.* Bantam Books. New York.

Covey, Stephen R. 1989. *The Seven Habits of Highly Effective People.* Simon and Schuster. New York.

Dugan, Timothy and Coles, Robert. 1989. *The Child in Our Times: Studies in the Development of Resiliency.* Brunner-Mazel. New York.

Gardner, Howard. 1983. *Frames of Mind: The Theory of Multiple Intelligences.* Basic Books, Inc. New York.

Garmezy, Norman. March/April, 1991. "Resilience and Vulnerability to Adverse Developmental Outcomes Associated with Poverty." *American Behavioral Scientist,* Volume 34, Number 4.

Garmezy, Norman and Rutter, Michael. 1983. *Stress, Coping and Development in Children*. McGraw-Hill. New York.

Glenn, H. Stephen. 1989. *Raising Self-Reliant Children in a Self-Indulgent World*. Sunrise Press, Fairoaks, CA

Hawkins, David, J., Catalano, Richard F., Miller, Janey Y. 1992. "Risk and Protective Factors for Alcohol and Other Drug Problems in Adolescence and Early Adulthood: Implications for Substance Abuse Programs." *Psychological Bulletin*. Volume 112, Number 1.

Healy, Jane M. 1990. *Endangered Minds: Why Children Don't Think and What We Can Do About It*. Touchstone Books, New York.

Healy, Jane M. 1987. *Your Child's Growing Mind*. Doubleday. New York.

Johnson, Virginia. March 1982. "Myelin and Maturation: A Fresh Look at Piaget" *The Science Teacher*, Volume 49, Number 3.

Kosaba, Suzanne, et al. 1985. "Effectiveness of Hardiness, Exercise and Social Support as Resources Against Illness." *Journal of Psychosomatic Research*. Volume 29, Number 5.

Louv, Richard. 1987. *Childhood's Future: Listening to the American Family—Hope and Solutions for the Next Generation*. Doubleday, New York.

McIntyre, K., White, D., and Yoast, R. 1990. *Resilience Among High Risk Youth*. University of Wisconsin-Madison. Wisconsin Clearinghouse.

Miller, Alice. 1990. *The Untouched Key: Tracing Childhood Trauma in Creativity and Destructiveness*. Doubleday, New York.

Pearce, Joseph Chilton. 1986. *The Magical Child Matures*. Bantam Books. New York.

Pearce, Joseph Chilton. 1992. *Evolution's End: Claiming the Potential of Our Intelligence*. Harper-Collins, San Francisco, CA

Peck, Scott. 1978. *The Road Less Traveled*. Touchstone Books, New York.

Phillips, Nancy. July, 1990. "Wellness During Adolescent Development." *Prevention Forum*, Vol. 10, No. 4.

Pittman, Karen J. September 30, 1991. "A New Vision: Promoting Youth Development." Testimony provided to the Congressional House Select Committee on Children, Youth and Family.

Richardson, Glenn E., et al. Nov/Dec 1990. "The Resiliency Model." *Health Education*.

Robertson, Joel C. June/July 1989. "Changing Self-Destructive Behavior in Adolescents Through Recreational Activities." *Adolescent Counselor*.

Rutter, Michael. March 1984. "Resilient Children." *Psychology Today*.

Rutter, Michael. 1985. "Resilience in the Face of Adversity: Protective Factors and Resistance to Psychiatric Disorder." *British Journal of Psychiatry*, Volume 147.

Schorr, Lisbeth. As quoted in "The Miracle of Resiliency." David Gelman. *Newsweek*. Volume 117, Number 1.

Segal, Julius. 1986. *Winning Life's Toughest Battles: Roots of Human Resilience*. McGraw-Hill, New York.

Seligman, Martin E. P. 1990. *Learned Optimism: How to Change Your Mind and Your Life*. Pocket Books, New York.

Werner, Emmy. April, 1989. "Children of the Garden Island." *Scientific American.*

Werner, Emmy. November 1984. "Resilient Children." *Young Children.* National Association for the Education of Young Children.

Werner, Emmy. 1982. *Vulnerable but Invincible: A Longitudinal Study of Resilient Children and Youth.* Adams, Bannister and Cox. New York.

Werner, Emmy. 1990. "Protective Factors and Individual Resilience." *Handbook of Early Childhood Intervention.* Cambridge University Press. Cambridge, New York.

Wolin, Steven J. and Sybil Wolin. 1993. *The Resilient Self: How Survivors of Troubled Families Rise Above Adversity.* Villard Books, New York.

Tim Burns' Video Tapes

Burns' video tapes are a complete set of training and educational videos for counsellors, teachers, parents, and caregivers to children. These eight video cassettes form a dynamic progression that first defines the basic physical and societal challenges confronting young people today, then examines child development from infancy to late childhood and adolescence, formalizes the empowering paradigm of resilience in the human spirit, and finally carries this touchstone into dynamic application. Thus Burns closes today's awful gulf between children and adults while reinforcing the basic principle that we must, ourselves, embody the characteristics and principles of resiliency in order to better model and practice the caregiving so necessary to the survival of our civilization.

Tim Burns' Books

Burns' second book, *Our Children, Our Future* (1991, 1992), his first with Marco Polo Publishers, is now in its second edition. This book describes the broad scope of developmental potential inherent in growing children—as that potential is understood across a number of disciplines, and acts as background for *Risk to Resilience*.

Tim Burns' Audio Tapes

Brain, Mind, and Spirit, Recorded live at the Governor's Summit for a Drug-Free Oklahoma, these audio tapes—with accompanying artwork—carefully substantiate Tim's findings by vast quantities of hard, scientific evidence. You'll listen to them again and again, discovering important new details and information each time you play them.

Words on Youth, is an exciting combination, in an attractive presentation box, of both Brain, Mind, and Spirit AND a second-edition copy of Our Children, Our Future. A must for care-providers who need to know WHY as well as HOW.

Phone Marco Polo Publishers at
1-800-743-7015
for more information

It's Easy to Order Tim Burns' Books, Video Tapes, and Audio Tapes

video title   how many   line $ total

BVT-251 Society at Risk @ 39.50
VIDEO TAPE

BVT-252 The Bonding Years @ 39.50
VIDEO TAPE

BVT-253 Early Childhood @ 39.50
VIDEO TAPE

BVT-254 Discovering Society @ 39.50
VIDEO TAPE

BVT-255 Risk to Resilience @ 39.50
VIDEO TAPE

BVT-256 The Resilient Child @ 39.50
VIDEO TAPE

BVT-25RS.1 Set of All SIX Tapes @ 199.00
6 VIDEO TAPES

BVT-257 Anatomy of a Crisis @ 49.50
VIDEO TAPE

BVT-258 Resilient Provider @ 49.50
VIDEO TAPE

BVT-25OS Anatomy, Provider BOTH @ 79.00
2 VIDEO TAPES

BB-10 Our Children, Our Future @ 15.00
BOOK

BB-11 From Risk to Resilience @ 15.00
BOOK

BAT-10 Brain, Mind, and Spirit @ 17.50
2 AUDIO TAPES WITH GRAPHICS

BC-10 Words on Youth @ 25.00
LIBRARY ALBUM: BOOK AND
AUDIO TAPES

line $ total

Order Total _____

Postage, packing, and handling (3.25/tape; 5.50 two or more) _____

Texas Residents (only) please add 8.25% sales tax _____

Total remitted _____

SECOND: to charge, please fill out the information below:

My name is: _____

My organization is: _____

My phone number is: _____

Ship to: _____
number   street or P.O. box

_____
code   city   state   zip

My VISA/MC # is: ____ / ____ / ____ / ____
circle one

Exp: ____ / ____
We'd Love To Have Your Business Card!

THIRD: PHONE OR MAIL YOUR ORDER

TO PHONE:
A. Dial our Toll-Free Order Line: 1-800-743-7015.
B. Read BOTH sides of this form at the voice prompt.

TO MAIL:
Simply detatch this order form, place in an envelope with a check made out to "MARCO POLO PUBLISHERS," and mail to:

the MARCO POLO PUBLISHERS
17194 Preston Road, Suite 123
Dallas, Texas 75248-1203

100 % Money-Back Guarantee

If you are not completely satisfied that the video tape's that you received are a valuable resource to you, simply return them within 30 days to receive a complete, 100% refund. No questions asked.

Marco Polo

You Can Send Purchase Orders On Our Fax Number:

Schools, treatment facilities, and governmental agencies . . . your purchase orders are welcome. Please insure that they have an original signature. Our terms are net 10 days from receipt of product. You may fax your order to (214) 424-1269; however, we will need a signed hard copy to follow.

Notes

Notes

Notes

About the Author

Tim Burns is a consultant, trainer, presenter, and university instructor with more than twenty years' experience with young people in recreational, educational, and therapeutic settings. This includes ten years' work in parenting education and family counseling. He is a former high school teacher, chemical dependency counselor, and adolescent substance abuse treatment program director. He holds a master's degree in counseling and is certified as both an alcoholism counselor and a clinical mental health counselor.

Tim has been a trainer with the New Mexico Substance Abuse Division since 1983 and an instructor for the University of New Mexico Alcohol and Drug Abuse Studies Program since 1987. He has taught undergraduate and graduate-level courses for the University of New Mexico in addiction studies, family studies, and parenting.

As a trainer and consultant, Tim has worked with more than 150 school districts and 250 agencies, groups, institutions, and professional associations. He has been on the faculty of numerous national and regional conferences and three international symposia related to high-risk youth, the family, and addiction.

Tim currently works extensively as a student assistance program consultant, core-team trainer, and as a frequent speaker at conferences and in communities around the nation. Tim also donates one day each week to work with a local school district, personally working with some of the at-risk students.

Tim is the author of the acclaimed *Anatomy of a Crisis: The Effects of Alcohol and Other Drugs on the Growing Brain, Mind, and Spirit*, published by Ginn Press in 1989 and *Our Children, Our Future: Defining the Stakes in a Battle We Must Not Lose*, published by Marco Polo Publishers in 1991 and 1992. He lives in Santa Fe, New Mexico, with his wife, Zana, a prevention specialist, and his daughters, Ashley and Megan.

Individuals or groups wishing to contact
the author for purposes of correspon-
dence, presentations, or training can
contact him, as follows:

E. Timothy Burns
c/o The Marco Polo Group
Marco Polo Publications
17194 Preston Road
Dallas, Texas 75248-1203